McFarland

Title: **The Muse Process**
Loc:
Author: Cox

Publication date: January 2019

Page Count: 213pp.

Binding: softcover

Price: $19.99

pISBN: 978-1-4766-7491-9

eISBN: 978-1-4766-3529-3

LC:

Publisher: McFarland – McFarlandBooks.com – 800-253-2187

This book is sent to you for review. We ask that our website
(McFarlandBooks.com) accompany the review and that the
publisher be listed as "McFarland" (one word). Send one copy of
the published review to publicist Beth Cox at bcox@mcfarlandpub.com.
If published online, please email a link to the review. For print media,
we prefer to receive a PDF file of the review emailed as an attachment.
(Hard-copy tearsheets, journals and magazines should be mailed to
Beth Cox, McFarland, Box 611, Jefferson NC 28640.)

The Muse Process

*Unleashing the Power of the Feminine
for Success and Fulfillment*

BARBARA COX

Exposit

Jefferson, North Carolina

ISBN (print) 978-1-4766-7491-9 ∞
ISBN (ebook) 978-1-4766-3529-3

LIBRARY OF CONGRESS CATALOGUING DATA ARE AVAILABLE

BRITISH LIBRARY CATALOGUING DATA ARE AVAILABLE

Front cover images © 2019 Shutterstock

Printed in the United States of America

Exposit is an imprint of McFarland & Company, Inc., Publishers

Exposit
Box 611, Jefferson, North Carolina 28640
www.expositbooks.com

To mitochondrial Eve

Table of Contents

Table of Contents

I am especially happy and thankful for finding a community in the Higher Vision choir, led by James Vandenburg. This community has been a breath of fresh air in my life. I truly value each and every one of you.

I wrote this book during a very difficult time in my life. Many turbulent shifts and changes were occurring in my life. My in-laws, who were dear parents to me, passed away during the writing of this book, as well as others who were dear to me. I kept plugging away on the writing. This book kept me going. I knew I needed to share these tools with the world at large, no matter what. So, I appreciate you, my dear readers, for reading these words.

Acknowledgments

I am overflowing with love and gratitude for my husband D. Cox for his sense of humor in this life journey and for my dear daugh. Delilah Cox in reminding me to take time out to enjoy life.

I am very grateful to my parents for having me, so that I can expe rience this time of great transformative change in history and be presen to write this book. I feel strongly that producing this book is my purpose in life and why I am here.

I am deeply grateful for the support I received from Christine Tomasello. Writing can be a lonely business and she was a lifeline to keep me going, so that I didn't feel I was in this by myself. She kept me going by reminding me too that this was an important message to get out into the world. In addition, she helped remind me to not put the metaphorical refrigerator in the bathroom while organizing the format of this book.

I give my heartfelt thanks to Dr. Michele Ritterman. Her presentations and trainings changed my life.

A big thank you to Beth Bolwerk for early editorial support.

I so appreciate my publisher Exposit for their friendly and organized office and especially for taking a chance on a newbie.

I also extend gratitude to Bill O'Hanlon, M.A., for his assistance in teaching me how to format my outline and proposal.

I am filled with thankfulness for the dear friends and family who stuck by me and supported me during this process of producing a book. I am especially grateful to my friend Rebecca Hill for introducing me to her friend Diana. This introduction led me to eventually finding my publisher.

I am thankful for my time as a civilian working for the Department of the Navy. I felt very valued and appreciated for my work there.

Preface

Note: All client examples used in this book are composites of several clients, with names and identifying information changed to protect privacy.

I believe there are two lives everybody leads. There's the life we have when we function on auto-pilot, guided by worry, fear, and lack. Then there's our authentic life—the one we are meant to lead, that requires us to push through the worry, conquer the fear, and choose a mindset of empowerment over disempowerment. When we live our authentic life, we are aligned with our highest values and live with purpose. This book, which outlines the Muse Process, will help guide you to your authentic life.

I wrote this self-help book following the birth of my daughter. At the time, I was working as a psychologist and executive coach helping women who were struggling with a sense of disconnection and invisibility. We focused on rediscovering their purpose in life, rediscovering the "spark" that drives them, and connecting to their "tribe" or some meaningful community. In doing this work, I became acutely aware of a pattern in my clients' lives—as they took on certain new roles, especially the roles of wife, partner, or mother, certain clients seemed to lose a sense of their individuality, which ignited their feelings of isolation and invisibility. After guiding them through this five-step Muse Process and witnessing their shift from hopeless and disengaged to empowered and seen, I felt compelled to address this emerging issue.

This book draws on the notion of the collective unconscious—a set of guiding principles that is passed down in society from generation to generation to us. We are born into these subconscious guiding principles that influence our individual choices, whether we know it or not.

Preface

It's deep, structural programming that we don't see, but that guides our feelings, decisions, and behaviors. We also have programming that we are aware of that we have learned from our interactions with our environment. Yet, even the beliefs and behaviors that we are conscious of and feel we can change easily are impacted by the collective unconscious.

This book is a transformational program that inspires women to step into a place of power at work and in their lives. The principles you will learn are healing tools for you in your relationships and your work. There is an inherent balance in nature between two energies—the masculine and the feminine. The feminine energy is intuitive and includes creativity, collaboration, and community. Today's world, however, is often built on a foundation of solely masculine energy, which centers on individualism, competition, and scarcity when not paired and balanced with the feminine energy. In our society, we tend to marginalize the female voice and presence, and give precedence to the male voice, to the detriment of us all.

Several research studies show that accessing and valuing the feminine traits of intuition, collaboration, and community, along with the masculine traits, has a transformative effect on both homes and workplaces. My process shows you how to value both archetypes and draw from the best of each. It reinstates a balance between the masculine and feminine traits, and reminds us of the value of the feminine energy. After guiding my clients through an innovative five-step process to activate the feminine traits in a more egalitarian fashion, and witnessing the powerful shift from hopeless and invisible to empowered and seen, I felt compelled to share this vital issue.

I noticed in my work with women that there was often an unspoken guiding principle in their lives that once they got married or partnered and/or had a baby, everything else in their life (career, friends, hobbies, connections to others) became low priority, and their overall well-being suffered. This was not a conscious decision the women made. Getting into these relationships activated an unconscious belief system based on the collective mindset, which altered their sense of self as a woman. Somehow the energy that was focused on career and other aspects of life got drawn away and all of it refocused on home and family to the exclusion of themselves. The book argues that this pattern is detrimental to their family as well. This book is written for these women.

My Background

I'm writing this book in part because of my history and my story as it plays out in the grander life drama of the roles women play in society. I was born at the height of the 60s. My father was a Navy pilot and my mother was a Southern belle who quit her job after she married my father. My parents were not part of the hippie cultural revolution or the woman's movement to equalize the roles of women in society at that time.

After my mother graduated high school in Arkansas, she took a well-paying secretarial job. I remember her telling me that if you didn't wear pantyhose or a girdle to work you would be fired. She enjoyed her work from what I can recall her saying, but in that era, women were expected to quit their jobs when they married and raise a family. After a year or so at her job, she met my father. As the story so often goes, she fell in love and had to make some difficult decisions. He was being transferred to a new military base, so he asked my mother to marry him and move. She accepted and quit her very well-paying job to move to a new state with my father.

During those many years, my mother worked as a stay-at-home mom to raise my siblings and me. Being a Navy family, we also found ourselves moving to a new city every couple of years. Some years, we would move every year. We basically had to pack and unpack boxes and set up a brand new house and create new friendships every one to two years. This made it difficult for my mother to maintain a network of friends, leaving her pretty isolated aside from her children. I am sure this was a difficult situation for both of my parents. After many turbulent years of marriage, my parents divorced. I was a teenager at the time of their divorce.

Due to various factors, my mother was basically left with no job connections and close to penniless. After having not been in the work-force for many, many years, it was very difficult for her to re-enter the job market. I watched her struggle to support us as I was growing up, and I vowed that would never happen to me.

I am certain that I am not the only one that this story applies to. I bet that many of you whose parents or grandparents were undergoing the massive social and cultural changes of the 60s and 70s were affected in similar ways. Think of my story as an Everywoman story of that era, as we leave that type of struggle behind to a new, more enlightened way of being as women and as a society.

It can be difficult as a society shifts to find our footing, but I think we are at an exciting crossroads where we can help redefine society in a way that works for all of us—women and men, so that we can come to an innate realization that our world does not have to be built solely on competition and scarcity—we can shift to a model that builds in cooperation and collaboration. This type of integrated model leads to a better functioning, more prosperous society.

Because of my life experience and the experience with my clients, I wrote this book to offer the tools and skills to other women to empower them. Even in this day and age as these types of struggles still happen, I feel my purpose in life is to help ensure that women have more options—to have a mindset that empowers them to have both an enjoy-able life and an enjoyable career. Hopefully, along the way, they will ditch the guilt that was a side effect of the old ways of thinking.

I will also present statistics that show how, when women are doing well economically, the whole world benefits—not just the women, not just their children, but men too, the white-collar man and the blue-collar man and everyone in between. The whole society benefits when women succeed. As Michael Kimmel states in his 2015 TED talk, research shows the more gender equal a nation is, the higher it rates on happiness measures. Similarly, the more gender equal an organization is, the higher the retention rates and employee satisfaction levels.[1]

It is my hope that this book creates change on two levels. I'd like to be the guide that shows how you, an individual, can help make your world a better place just by adopting some of these balanced mindsets that say I can have a happy life and a happy career. And I wish for this book to prompt policy changes in our society that engender an easier path for women entering (or re-entering) the workforce. For organizations to realize, after reading this book, that hiring and retaining women helps their bottom line, and concretely helps the men in those organizations as well as their surrounding communities.

Please join me on this journey for a more empowered society for you and your loved ones.

The Muse Process

Below is a summary of the Muse Process that you will learn. Don't worry; I'll lead you through it all.

1. **DEFINE**—*Uncovering Your Goals:* Craft a short phrase to **define** and "feel" your desired life vision—your goal—in the present tense. You will learn this in Chapter 1.

2. **VISION**—*Relaxed Alpha State:* Learn to get into a relaxed "alpha" **meditative state** to actualize your life **vision**. There are many ways to do this and I will teach you some options throughout the following chapters so you can pick one that resonates with you and practice it. You will learn this in Chapters 2 and 3.

3. **ACT**—*Getting Results by Taking Action:* **Follow any action steps** or **insights** you get while in the relaxed alpha state. You will learn this in Chapters 4 and 5.

4. **CONNECT**—*Cultivating Collaboration:* As you relax and open space in your life, you are most open to helpful change and positive patterns—including shifting old roles and adopting new roles. Cultivate a **collaborative community** that supports these positive changes. You will learn this in Chapters 6 and 7.

5. **NEUTRALIZE**—*Using Neutrality to Create Change:* Develop the skill of **neutrality** to avoid getting pulled off your path or goal. You will learn this in Chapter 8.

Preface

I will introduce you to these tools and illustrate them with real-life cases to help you realize that whatever challenges you face in your life—be they old belief patterns, stress, money concerns, job transitions, or other issues—you can, through the power of your mind, be the master of your own destiny. It may not happen tomorrow, but if you stay on the path, you can and will achieve great things. Ready?

REFERENCES

1. Kimmel, M. (2015, May). *Why gender equality is good for everyone—men included* [video file]. Retrieved from https://www.ted.com/talks/michael_kimmel_why_gender_equality_is_good_for_everyone_men_included.

CHAPTER 1

Finding Your Inner Success Muse— Your Mental App for Success

"Step out of the history that is holding you back. Step into the new story you are willing to create."—Oprah Winfrey

This chapter will give an overview of the Muse Process and the Muse Effect. You will get a first introduction to your inner success Muse—the archetype or program inside you that we will activate during the five-step process in the book that leads you to a life of creative fulfillment and joy. This includes having fulfilling relationships (be they with spouses, colleagues, children, family, or friends), fulfillment at work and in your career, and passion for life overall.

In my work as a coach, I have seen countless clients go from stressed and unhappy to living a happy and fulfilling life. Many groups or individuals that contact me for training seek a healthy work-life balance. The term work-life balance can be a pleasant way to say, "We're stressed out, please teach us how to clear out this stress and live a fulfilling, happy life." In the past, I used this five-step process with clients in individual coaching sessions, and have now developed it as a self-guided process to help you make the same journey.

The tools you will learn during this process are innovative mindset-management tools designed to get you to where you want to be. They will assist you in going from confusion and stagnation to clarity and freedom in your life, so you can enjoy applying your talents and also have the courage to be an agent of change in your world. And furthermore, we spend so much time at work, why not create permission to be happy, calm, and prosperous while we're there as well?

To make the information even easier to absorb, I have included an outline at the beginning of each chapter to serve as a roadmap of what you will learn in that chapter before we dive right in.

Here is the roadmap showing what you will learn in Chapter 1.

- Overview: What Is the Five-Step Muse Process?
- What Are the Conscious Mind and the Unconscious Mind?
- Case Study—Jennifer and Her Dream Job
- Practice—Relaxed Breathing Activity
- Practice—Envision Your Ideal Work-Life Situation
- Practice—Lock In Your Life Vision
- Our Mind as an Upgradable App

OVERVIEW: WHAT IS THE FIVE-STEP MUSE PROCESS?

The Muse Process is a five-step creative process that will align your conscious and unconscious mind with your goals and help them all work together to build a more successful life that flows more easily—including work, relationships, and family connections. I use the word Muse to describe the old cultural stories of a personified force, usually feminine, which is a source of inspiration and motivation in your life. Muse originates from the old French word *muser*, which means to meditate.

The Muse Effect is the product of implementing the Muse Process. It is the flowing balance in life that happens when you honor and integrate your conscious and unconscious mind to work together. Then, life works better for you and for those around you. Make sense?

To review, here is a summary of the process that you'll be learning. This process is designed to align your life wishes with your unconscious and conscious mind so that they work together. I am simplifying it here again as a template, so that you are able to learn it rather easily as you read and absorb the material in this book:

1. **DEFINE**—*Uncovering Your Goals:* Craft a short phrase to **define** and "feel" your desired life vision—your goal—in present tense. You will learn this in Chapter 1.

2. **VISION**—*Relaxed Alpha State:* Learn to get into a relaxed "alpha" **meditative state** to actualize your life **vision**. There are many ways to do this and I will teach you some options throughout the following chapters, so you can pick one that resonates with you and practice it. You will learn this in chapters 2 and 3.

3. **ACT**—*Getting Results by Taking Action:* **Follow any action steps** or **insights** you get while in the relaxed alpha-state. You will learn this in Chapters 4 and 5.

4. **CONNECT**—*Cultivating Collaboration:* As you relax and open space in your life, you are most open to helpful change and positive patterns—including shifting old roles and adopting new roles. Cultivate a **collaborative community** that supports these positive changes. You will learn this in Chapters 6 and 7.

5. **NEUTRALIZE**—*Using Neutrality to Create Change:* Develop the skill of **neutrality** to avoid getting pulled off your path or goal. You will learn this in Chapter 8.

I know this process might seem like a lot of information at this point, but don't worry ... this book covers each step of the process thoroughly and guides you in a very clear way. Plus, I've written the book so that even if you do not think you remember the process exactly, your unconscious mind can absorb the information and you will see helpful changes in the way you approach daily life.

WHAT ARE THE CONSCIOUS MIND AND THE UNCONSCIOUS MIND?

As we go through the five-step process, I will sometimes use the words "unconscious" mind and "conscious" mind. I clarify what these terms mean in this section, since they are very powerful concepts. Some of you may find these two concepts easy to grasp. Some may not. In fact, scientists argued over the definition of these terms for many years and eventually some clear and simple definitions emerged. However, there are still some various interpretations. For simplicity, we will use these common definitions, which are all very similar.

Source	Definition of the Unconscious Mind	Definition of the Conscious Mind
Wikipedia[1,2]	*The unconscious mind (or the unconscious) consists of the processes in the mind which occur automatically and are not available to introspection, and include thought processes, memories, interests, and motivations.*	*Consciousness is the state or quality of awareness, or of being aware of an external object or something within oneself. It has been defined variously in terms of sentience, awareness, qualia, subjectivity, the ability to experience or to feel, wakefulness, having a sense of selfhood or soul.*
Dictionary.com[3,4]	*The unconscious, Psychoanalysis. The part of the mind containing psychic material that is only rarely accessible to awareness but that has a pronounced influence on behavior.*	*The conscious, Psychoanalysis. The part of the mind comprising psychic material of which the individual is aware.*
My definition	*The intuitive part of the mind that works outside of our awareness.*	*The logical, analytic part of our mind that is inside of our awareness.*

What Are the Conscious Mind and the Unconscious Mind?

In essence,

- **The unconscious mind = the intuitive mind**
- **The conscious mind = the analytic mind**

Just know that the unconscious is the part of the mind we are normally unaware of—the intuitive mind. The conscious is the part of the mind we are aware of—the analytic mind.

Here is a humorous personal story about the conscious and unconscious mind and how they work, to illustrate the point in more detail for you. My business manager, Christine, had been working with me for about four years, and during that time we had always met on Tuesdays at 10 a.m. for our weekly meeting.

One week, due to some unforeseen circumstance, we had to change our weekly meeting from Tuesday at 10 a.m. to Friday at 11 a.m. On the Friday morning of our meeting, Christine walked in laughing and said that she had a funny story to tell me.

She told me that she knew we were meeting that week at 11 a.m. on Friday. She had it on her calendar, and had even put a sticky note on her mirror in the bathroom to remind her of the change. She consciously was aware of making a schedule change. But on Tuesday morning, she got in her car to run an errand and found herself in front of the office at 10 a.m.! She looked around for a second, wondering why she was there. And then she realized—even though her conscious mind knew we weren't meeting that day, her unconscious mind didn't realize that and it led her to my office on Tuesday at 10 a.m.—our normal meeting time! Her unconscious mind, the part of her that holds regular reflexes and habits, took over and brought her to my office.

This story shows how, even though you make a plan to do something consciously, if you have a regular habit, such as meeting weekly, that habit is stored in your unconscious mind. The unconscious mind is the storehouse for reflexes and automatic behavior, things we don't think of consciously. The unconscious mind stores reflexes and such so that we do not have to waste time thinking about every single thing. It is kind of like an efficiency shortcut. However, sometimes these reflexes can cause an override of a conscious plan if they are very regularly ingrained, such as our weekly Tuesday meeting (four years is a long time and it developed a strong reflex).

This situation with Christine happened because her unconscious patterns, her regular habits, overrode her conscious plan. Her conscious mind was offline, so to speak. This illustrates the power of the unconscious mind. That's why it is important to know the definition of unconscious and conscious and to work with both parts … so that you can teach them to work together and collaborate for your happiness in life.

We are also going to integrate the unconscious and conscious aspects of the mind that some philosophies refer to as the yin and yang elements of us. Let's think of yin as the receptive, intuitive part of us and yang as the more action-oriented and analytic part of us. Some of these philosophies say that yin elements of human nature include the feminine elements and that the yang is associated with the masculine elements. It posits that each of us has both yin and yang elements and that a whole and balanced person honors both the masculine and the feminine elements within—we are speaking of these elements based on the qualities they contain, regardless of gender. I am simplifying this concept for our purposes in order for us to connect with all the helpful parts of our psyche—we, as balanced and whole individuals, can activate both parts of us, the receptive, intuitive part and the action-oriented, analytic part, regardless of gender. So, along this line of thinking, some of the personality functions traditionally associated with the feminine qualities are intuition, community, and collaboration. Throughout this book, we are going to set up a template to honor and bring those in to our everyday world and integrate them with the more "masculine" associated functions of the mind, such as logic and individualism.

The unconscious mind can do some pretty amazing things. It can also throw in reflexive habits that we didn't plan for. Sometimes, as the above example illustrates, we may have the best consciously laid out plans and they go awry. At times during our daily life, we may wonder, "Why did this plan not work?" or "Why do I keep on repeating the same mistakes and patterns over and over?" Sometimes, we may throw up our hands in disgust and wonder if the world is out to get us. We may try to enact a plan for change and then feel it's not working. Oftentimes, that is because you have not uncovered what your unconscious mind wants. Or, it may not want anything at all that is unknown or mysterious. You may have just gotten into an unconscious habit that is no longer relevant to the current circumstances. Like a knee-jerk reaction, you may be repeating a pattern, just like Christine did. It's not that the old habit was bad. It may have served a purpose to help you in the past, maybe when you were a child or a baby, even. It may have been an old habit you picked up unknowingly from you mom or dad or teacher or boss or neighbor. Old habits can be extracted and replaced with new, more current ones.

Some of this stuff is going to blow your mind. Some of it you may have heard previously. Sometimes, oddly enough, changing old subconscious patterns to something more up to date can activate a feeling of irritation or anger. That is because when your body is used to something, it may feel uncomfortable to change it. I liken it to working out. If you start a new workout routine, some muscles may not be used to it and will feel a bit achy or irritated for a day, even though a bit of exercise is healthy for you. Some of the information may bother you because it discusses the intersection of feminism and biology. All of it is going to help you. But let's get it out of the way now—take a minute to say aloud, "Barbara, this is pissing me off!" There, now we can move forward to help the unconscious align with the conscious mind and pave a new frontier for you.

How the Unconscious Mind Works in Parallel with the Conscious Mind

There is some surprising new research that illustrates very clearly that there is an unconscious mind which does a lot of the heavy grunt work in solving problems. Most of us know that, if I reach for an apple, my hand moves to the apple and grasps my fingers around it in an automatic way. I do not have to consciously think about how to wrap my fingers around that apple. It automatically happens. If I drive to my house, I really do not have to consciously think about how to drive my car. I just get in and drive and all the steps in between, including turning on the ignition, backing up, pressing the gas pedal, just flow.

As I mentioned earlier, there was a long-term discussion in psychology about what is done by the unconscious, and what requires conscious thought. In the past, it was widely believed that the unconscious only performs simple reflexive behaviors, like muscle memory. Sometimes, it was inferred that the unconscious was rather dumb or reactive and that the conscious mind was the smart one. A recent experiment by researchers Asael Sklar and colleagues shows otherwise.[5] This research team was able to show that we are in fact able to process multiple word expressions and solve math equations outside of our conscious awareness! They used a wonderful visual trick called Continuous Flash Suppression in this experiment. In a nutshell, Continuous Flash Suppression uses light-bending glasses to show people different images in each eye. One eye gets a succession of brightly colored flashing squares in order to distract the study participant and that causes the participant to not be consciously aware of the information that is presented to the other eye. The researchers presented complex arithmetic to the unconscious mind in order to determine how "smart" it was, asking in effect, "Do we need to solve all complex problems with the conscious mind?" The answer in short is no. Some complex problems can be solved by our unconscious mind.

The arithmetic problems solved by the unconscious mind were surprisingly complex. The questions involved complex arithmetic such as 9 −3 −4 = ___. I have included the full details of the study in the notes at the end of the chapter if you would like to read about it in more detail.

This realization that the unconscious can do more than we previously thought is a very powerful realization as we work through this book. Sometimes, let your unconscious do your heavy lifting, OK?

Think of the mind as a beautiful iceberg. The unconscious mind is like the vast potential of the underwater part of the iceberg, and the conscious mind is the seen tip of the iceberg. We are just beginning to learn what is below the tip of the iceberg. Throughout this book, you will learn ways to harness the power of both your unconscious and conscious mind.

Now that we are getting familiar with the conscious and unconscious mind and what amazing things our minds are capable of, let's talk about how this can benefit you in your daily life. We'll start by learning how one of my clients used the power of her mind for helpful change, and then I'll show you how you can too.

CASE STUDY— JENNIFER AND HER DREAM JOB

The best introduction to the Muse Process is summarized in the following case study. (Remember, I've changed the names and identifying details to protect clients' privacy.) As I was heartened by this client's results, I began to systematize the process with hundreds of future clients. This story explains how following just a few steps can positively change your mental state and open you up to a happier life.

Jennifer called me because she was feeling frustrated and anxious with her work situation. She had originally worked in a large metropolitan city prior to being transferred by her company to a smaller, more sedate city. Her new position was high-pressured and it entailed long hours. She was unhappy with the transition. In the first three sessions, we primarily explored what things about her work duties she enjoyed and what in her prior work and life felt happy and fulfilling. We wove in some exploration of what happy work would feel like. When I taught her some relaxation tools during the fourth session, we explored what a happy, fulfilling work environment and life looked like, as if she was already in it. I accomplished this by having her play a game with her mind, imagining going to her near future and seeing herself in her optimal work environment and life, with an enjoyable workplace as well as enjoyable relationships. *In essence, we created a template where enjoyable work and relationships—where significant other, co-workers, colleagues, friends, and family all felt supportive to her unfolding life vision.*

Creating a Path for Optimal Work

My goal was to help her create or access a mental, subconscious filter for "happy, prosperous work and life" so that she would have a gut feeling of what that felt like. Then she was more likely to naturally gravitate to the action steps she needed to take or people she needed to contact to make that imagined scene a concrete reality. I had her go on a mental journey in a relaxed meditative state, and when she completed that mental journey, we discussed in more detail what she had seen and felt. She clearly described the types of people she was with, what work she was doing, how much money she was making, and she saw herself in a different city, one that was more metropolitan and high powered. She realized what key factors were important to her in her life. We also explored any action steps she felt called to take.

She committed to do the simple action steps of contacting certain people that had popped into her mind during the sessions, along with practicing the tools. About seven months later, she came in for another session. She was ecstatic, saying, "It happened just like I envisioned in our last session: I got the job I wanted in the city I wanted, and I'm moving next month!" What was even more exciting was that her new position had a higher salary. In future chapters, we'll follow other case studies as we create a template where enjoyable work and relationships—i.e., where significant other, co-workers, colleagues, friends, and family all feel supportive to our unfolding life vision as well.

As you can see from this case study, the power of the mind is incredible. If you learn to trust it and use it to your benefit, you can achieve amazing things. Instead of working "bottom-up"—i.e., going from the details to the big picture—learn to work "top-down" by creating your big-picture mental filter. This process weeds out busy work in life, thereby making life less anxiety provoking. We have way too much needless busy-ness in life as a culture. If you have a purpose for your life that you focus on, you can weed out the anxiety-producing, needless busyness.

In the next section, I will walk you through the same steps I did with Jennifer and show you the basics of learning to be in a relaxed, meditative state called an alpha state. Be prepared to define your goals and be open to understanding a different side to yourself. We will start with a little practice to get you in a relaxed state of mind and a visualization practice to start to develop your own personalized vision for your ideal work and life.

PRACTICE—
RELAXED BREATHING ACTIVITY

To start step one on our journey, we are going to learn a basic technique that develops more relaxed breathing and gets you ready for learning the next steps of our process. This is one of the first tools I teach my clients. All the case studies, including Jennifer's above, start with this simple practice and go from there.

If you like to relax by lying down, version A is for you. If you like to relax by walking, version B is for you.

Version A

Our breathing pattern can be more noticeable when we are lying down and in a quiet location.

So if you are able, lie comfortably on the floor, place one hand on your upper chest and the other hand on your belly.

For now, breathe how you normally would and notice which hand rises and falls the most.

If you are currently tense or anxious, you tend to breathe from the chest with short, shallow breaths.

If you notice that you are breathing from the chest, begin to move your attention to your belly and notice the weight of your hand there.

Place both hands on your abdomen.

Begin inhaling through your nose, slowly, and imagine that you are completely filling your lungs with air so that the lungs push out your abdomen.

You feel this push on your hands and exhale slowly through your mouth while noticing the movement of the abdomen. Breathe in this manner for a few minutes, inhaling through your nose and exhaling through your mouth, and allow your breathing to relax and slow down even more. To simplify it even more: Just be curious about the air reaching the lowest point of your belly. Do this for however long you wish. A few minutes are just fine. However long you decide is just fine.

Version B

If you relax by movement, you can do the same relaxed breathing activity while walking somewhere peaceful and quiet—for example, the beach, or the woods, or outside of your house. I will modify the exercise just a tiny bit to allow for movement:

We are going to learn a basic technique that develops relaxed breathing and gets you ready for learning the next steps of our process.

So as you begin walking, gently place one hand on your upper chest and the other hand on your belly.

For now, just breathe how you normally would and notice which hand rises and falls the most.

If you are currently tense or anxious, you tend to breathe from the chest with short, shallow breaths.

If you notice that you are breathing from the chest, begin to move your attention to your belly and notice your hand there. Just notice and be curious.

Place both hands on your abdomen.

Begin inhaling through your nose, slowly, and imagine that you are completely filling your lungs with air so that the lungs push out your abdomen.

You may feel this push on your hands and exhale slowly through your mouth while noticing the movement of the abdomen. Breathe in this manner for a few minutes, inhaling through your nose and exhaling through your mouth. I invite you to allow your breathing to relax and slow down even more. As you are walking, I invite you to now just let your hands drop to your sides and walk at your normal pace, and just be curious about the air reaching the lowest point of your belly. Do this for however long you wish. A few minutes are just fine. However long you decide is just fine.

If you would like a short audio version of this to listen to, visit my website at www.drbarbaracox.com.

PRACTICE— ENVISION YOUR IDEAL WORK-LIFE SITUATION

Now that you are even more relaxed, let's play a game.

Part One

Imagine that when you go to sleep tonight, a magical mist sweeps over you and you wake up to your ideal work-life situation. You have exactly what you want in regard to work—and it flows with the rest of your life too. What is it? Really play the game and imagine having exactly what you want. Allow yourself to have it.

Describe the scenario in your own words below (don't worry about the exact wording; just write it down as it comes to you):

Part Two

To activate this beneficial scenario even more in your unconscious mind, describe the following:

How are you feeling in this scenario you've just described?

What do you look like in that place?

What are you wearing?

What is one thing you are saying?

What are you eating for lunch?

What is something you smell in this scenario?

How do others respond to you?

Who is one person that most supports you here?

Who is most helpful to you here?

EXAMPLE

Let's follow along with Jennifer's response to the exercise to see how it helped her create positive shifts.

Part One

Imagine that when you go to sleep tonight, a magical mist sweeps over you and you wake up to your ideal work-life situation. You have exactly what you want in regard to work—and it flows with the rest of your life too. What is it? Really play the game and imagine having exactly what you want. Allow yourself to have it.

Describe the scenario in your own words below (don't worry about the exact wording; just write it down as it comes to you):

I've finally got my MBA and I've started my own successful start-up company, with flexible hours, a good amount of freedom, the opportunity to expand the company, and the opportunity to travel. I've purchased a great apartment in the middle of the city. I love it there. My boyfriend decides to move in and we become closer. My friends and I spend a lot of time making the most of living downtown, and my family comes to visit me and my boyfriend often (especially because I have a guest room for them to stay in!). I'm able to explore different creative outlets for myself, and I have the time and money to really dive in to them. I have a good, trusting relationship with friends, family, co-workers, and my boyfriend.

Part Two

To activate that even more, now describe:

How are you feeling in this scenario you've just described? *I'm motivated to do well at work, and am excited about my current job, social, and relationship status. I also feel free to pursue what I want in my free time, which makes me feel relaxed, inspired, and engaged in life.*

What do you look like in that place? *Well put-together, creative, healthy, and active.*

What are you wearing? *Comfortable, relaxed clothing with a professional twist.*

What is one thing you are saying? *I feel alive.*

What are you eating for lunch? *I'm eating a home-cooked meal at a friend's home with my boyfriend.*

What is something you smell in this scenario? *I smell curry and rice.*

How do others respond to you? *With respect, friendliness, openness, and a willingness to share their lives. They respond with more reciprocity.*

Who is one person that most supports you here? *My boyfriend feels very supportive.*

Who is most helpful to you here? *My whole community feels very supportive here.*

PRACTICE— LOCK IN YOUR LIFE VISION

In the above exercise, you described in detail your ideal life, especially focusing on your work situation and how your life supports that—in essence, the life vision you are completing in completing this book. Now, we are going to define your life vision with laser focus. Do this by describing your vision in nine words or less and write it in the present tense as if it has already happened in your life. That is why it is named "Lock in Your Life Vision"—because you see it transpiring in your life now. You will refer back to this vision often throughout the book.

If you are wondering why I recommend nine words or less, many studies show that the average person can hold about five to nine words in their short-term memory.

Write your statement here:

Some people might know right away what their vision statement is. Other people may find themselves unsure of what to say or sitting with a blank slate. If you find yourself in the second camp, I have provided some examples for you below. But before you read them, I invite you to try coming up with a couple of test statements first.

Keep in mind that one objective of this book is to help you tap into your unconscious skills in new ways. I invite you to be curious about what your unconscious mind comes up with for this exercise ... maybe even follow this curiosity for a day or two before crafting your statement for the Lock in Your Life Vision exercise. You are also welcome to change your statement midway through the book.

Write your statement here:

Here are a few examples my clients have come up with in our work together:

I am worthy of a harmonious life.

I am deserving of a harmonious life.

It's safe to have a harmonious life.

I am open to a harmonious life.

I can find joy in work and life now.

I am open to enjoyable work and supportive relationships.

I have enjoyable work and supportive relationships.

Wow, my life is great!

I am worthy of love, joy, and happiness.

I have love, peace, and connection in my life.

1. Finding Your Inner Success Muse

My life is filled with fun and engaging experiences.

I live life in a state of ease and flow.

My life and work flow well.

I have arrived.

I feel good with the balance in my life.

I have time, security, and motivation.

I am relaxed and calm more often.

EXAMPLE

Let's go back to Jennifer's example. Here is what she wrote for this exercise:

My life vision is…

I have happy, prosperous work.

Now it's your turn to lock in your vision:

My life vision is…

As we go through the exercises in the book, think of the process as if you were learning how to do something fun for the first time, like riding a bicycle or driving a car. As you review your life vision, it can be like that. Remember the moment you got your first bike? It was probably exciting and new. When you got onto the bicycle, it may have felt strange or wobbly. You might have even doubted you could balance at all. I bet you were still having fun with it even though it was new territory.

When we treat new learning or new experiences just like riding a bike, we can keep it light and fun. You kept at it because it was an exciting challenge. Heck, you may have even scratched your knee, but the bike called you forward, so you didn't even notice the knee. Some of you may have caught on quickly and others may have taken a little more time. Some of you probably kept your training wheels on for a long time—I know I did. But I bet you practiced a little bit day by day, because you were enjoying the process.

Think of this process like learning to ride your bike. You'll get on and, at the beginning, you may feel uncertain. You may feel excited. You will get back on when you wobble and then you keep going, just because it's fun and the wind is streaming in your hair. Imagine you are riding that bike now, laughing and having fun. I am here to cheer you on. Remember, once you learned the bike (or the car) it became an easy habit and went into your muscle memory or unconscious mind.

Everything you will learn here has the potential to go into your automatic memory so that it becomes second nature to you. Life can flow. You can release any struggle and learn a more helpful and balanced way. I am not saying to just program yourself to think life is super easy and let's just lay around eating bon-bons. That would be boring anyway. Well, you may try it for a short time and then decide it's boring. What I am saying is that life can be simpler. When we focus on doing what we love and allow ourselves to have a little bit of joy and pleasure in life, life is simpler then. It may even surprise you. You may look back on your life after you have learned these tools and say, hey, why was I so hard on myself before?

The philosophy included here is one of healthy living that includes fun and pleasure as an important part of life. It is reminding you to let yourself have the permission to enjoy healthy pleasures in life—to set your goal to enjoy life. I believe one of the main reasons we have problems in our society today stems from our collective Puritan background that basically secretly tells us life is hard and don't enjoy yourself. Oftentimes, we carry certain subconscious collective beliefs like this. Whether we are aware of it or not, many of us carry in our mind-body system a cultural puritanical belief pattern that says, "It's bad to enjoy the fun of life."

Over time, if we do not consciously address this belief and shift it, problems can arise. Our biology is hard-wired to enjoy healthy, pleasurable experiences in life—good food, riding our bikes, the pleasures of company and friends, and being in the body. If we deny ourselves these things, life can go awry.

When we get to a place of giving ourselves permission to enjoy healthy, pleasurable experiences and creating surroundings that encourage that—for example, beautiful, natural scenery, good food and taking time to enjoy it, chatting with friends—life becomes more rich and, paradoxically, we are able to work better and produce better results. When we learn the skill of healthy pleasures, life in all its facets—work, money, relationships, health—becomes easier and flows. That is something I know is important to all of us. So, get on your bike, metaphorically speaking, and let's have fun while you lock in your life vision.

OUR MIND
AS AN UPGRADABLE APP

Another metaphor I like to use is that of our mind as a computer app. It has various programs that you can choose to run, like the life vision program above, or delete if they are not helpful. It is really that simple. Let's explore this metaphor of how you can upgrade the app of your mental computer.

My system posits that we are like human computers in a way, where we have deep programming that's usually unseen to us—like our computers' operating system. We don't often look at the code that runs our computer but we know something is behind the scenes running it. It's deep, structural programming that runs our lives, just like our computers run without us having to program them. This operating system guides much of our mindset. This is a helpful metaphor in that you use these things probably daily—and you do not have to understand the technical workings of your computer to know that it comes with a built-in operating system that runs it.

You also know how to search for a useful app to do things for you to make your life easier. That is a lot of what you will be doing—upgrading your mental app. When you use your phone, you do not have to be a technical expert to use it. It is the same with learning the tools in this book. You can learn to upgrade your mental apps and you do not need to be an engineer to do it. Again, enjoy the process and make it simple.

Our Mind as an Upgradable App

Think of the last time you bought a computer, laptop, or phone. You took it out of the box and plugged it in and basically just hit the power button. The basic stuff just runs. The programming or operating system that runs your phone or computer without you having to think about it is part of you that is preprogrammed or was built in when you were born.

This includes what is called the collective unconscious—a set of guiding principles that you inherited in your operating system from the collective or your ancestors. As you matured into adulthood, the things you learned from school, friends, immediate family, and the environment are like new apps or software you downloaded to add to the basic information that was built in.

These are the things we'll be working with—the deep operating system and the more obvious apps and folders. And we'll be addressing how to shift your own individual experience of how you interpret your culture and the passed-down beliefs you had inadvertently inherited from the culture, and update your system so it's operating on the most up-to-date app. You will get the chance to go into the app store of life and choose apps that, for instance, install a more balanced and flowing view of work and partnerships. That's the app I want readers to download from reading this book.

Some of the old apps we'll be looking at and inviting you to change include the unconscious collective cultural belief that once you have kids or get married, everything else in your life has to suffer. By bringing awareness to these systems, other models will shift in your operating system too.

You can keep this metaphor of an app simple. Just remember, every time you find a helpful app on your phone or computer, you can give your subconscious mind the suggestion that it can upgrade to a happier way of being too. These metaphors are really about finding a clear and simple way for you as a woman to upgrade your life app to be happy with work and a balance of relationships.

We as a culture are moving away from an old app. This old app had women structure our subconscious in such a way that we did not consciously realize we were putting our partner and/or our children above ourselves at all costs, and our work or career became a distant third. That was the old app that we are in the process of changing. When I discuss this with friends and clients, we are always amazed that this app or pattern is so prevalent in observing other friends and themselves in relationships. They often feel it is a struggle to find balance between their work and relationships.

The tools in the following chapter will build on the metaphor of the bike as a flowing journey in life, the spokes in the wheel of life— you as a woman, your partner, friendships, children, family, and career— in a dynamic equilibrium as you ride through life, putting yourself in the center of your wheel. I myself have a child and a spouse and work, so when I originally wrote this, even I felt my subconscious knee-jerk reaction say, "Oh, that's so controversial." But think about it … is it really?

Even in an emergency, 32,000 feet in the air on a plane, the flight attendants tell us to put on our *own* oxygen mask before helping anyone else. They understand that we have to care for ourselves before we care for our kids or our partners (or even our pets). So why do we struggle to understand that?

As I sat and looked this issue originally, discussing it first with friends and later with clients, I heard a nagging voice in the back of my head berate the idea. "You can't put yourself first … that's so selfish … what will people think?!?" This is the voice of the old paradigm that is falling away. We are moving to a system where we need to realize that we need to put on our oxygen mask first and then we can help others. We need to allow a gentle balance in our life which allows more flow. I am not advocating a system of competition and pure selfishness, but one that recognizes the needs of women as both individuals and an interconnected part of society.

I realized in discussing this issue with my friends that we had hit upon an important issue, one that needed to be addressed in a conscious and aware manner. My friends and I always noticed that the healthiest and happiest women we knew that had partners and children and jobs and that were healthy and happy as well had reached some sort of dynamic equilibrium and balance. These women did put themselves first in their own internal universe. They had learned to ride their bike through life and somehow had upgraded their mental app to include a more balanced view of themselves and their world.

As we wrap up this chapter, we have identified your ideas of happiness and defined goals for your life. In the next chapter, you will learn how to reach a relaxed, meditative alpha state to help you reach your goals in life a bit easier.

••

KEY TAKE-AWAYS

✓ The first key for this chapter of the book: *just be curious about the air reaching the lowest point of your belly.*

✓ The second key for this chapter of the book: *practice the Lock in Your Vision activity to create a template for an enjoyable life.*

REFERENCES

1. Consciousness. (n.d.). In *Wikipedia*. Retrieved from https://en.wikipedia.org/wiki/Consciousness.

2. Unconscious mind. (n.d.). In *Wikipedia*. Retrieved from https://en.wikipedia.org/wiki/Unconscious_mind.

3. Conscious. (n.d.). In Dictionary.com. Retrieved from http://www.dictionary.com/browse/conscious?s=ts.

4. Unconscious. (n.d.). In Dictionary.com. Retrieved from http://www.dictionary.com/browse/unconscious?s=t.

5. Sklar, A.Y., Levy, N., Goldstein, A., Mandel, R., Maril, A., & Hassin, R.R. (2012). Reading and doing arithmetic unconsciously. *Proceedings of the National Academy of Sciences of the United States of America, 109*(48), pp. 19614–19619.
Note: In their abstract, the researchers stated that "the questions involved complex arithmetic such as '9 – 3 – 4 =___'" presented unconsciously during the distracting flashing lights and that would be followed by the presentation, fully visible, of a target number that the participants were asked to read aloud as quickly as possible. The target number could either be the correct answer to the arithmetic question ("2") or a wrong answer (for example, "1"). The results showed that study participants were significantly quicker to read the target number when it was the correct answer rather than a wrong answer. This result shows that the equation had been processed and solved by their unconscious minds—since they had no conscious awareness of an equation being presented. In the above abstract or summary link, the researchers state that "the modal view in the cognitive and neural sciences holds that consciousness is necessary for abstract, symbolic, and rule-following computations. Hence, semantic processing of multiple-word expressions, and performing of abstract mathematical computations, are widely believed to require consciousness. We report a series of experiments in

1. Finding Your Inner Success Muse

which we show that multiple-word verbal expressions can be processed outside conscious awareness and that multistep, effortful arithmetic equations can be solved unconsciously. The results show that novel word combinations, in the form of expressions that contain semantic violations, become conscious before expressions that do not contain semantic violations, that the more negative a verbal expression is, the more quickly it becomes conscious, and that subliminal arithmetic equations prime their results. These findings call for a significant update of our view of conscious and unconscious processes."

ed Alpha State =
ditative State

on of thoughts in Eternal awareness or
objectification, knowing without think-
ity."—Voltaire

hat an alpha state is, how it benefits
asily.

f relaxed, peaceful awareness that
a certain frequency of wavelength.
ling biofeedback, self-hypnosis,
echniques. People often ask me
state, guided imagery, self-
d meditation. I find that since
core, they are the same thing

a simplified definition.
meditative state or alpha
efine *meditative state* or
vareness that all people
own it is a natural state
our day. Therefore, it
cess is *self*-directed,
ctly what you want
you'll apply them

n Chapter 2.

ral state of
nd me, can

time, even if
a meditative
laxed state on
ially if you are
nd not remem-
on "auto pilot."
scious mind was
lpha state. I will
erchangeably.
you're in a relaxed
orcement. You can
through, for exam-
narios in a calm and
with these tools, you
ur daily interactions
ming your conscious
lly propel you toward
eve your goals.

2. Relaxed Alpha State = Meditative State

- What Is a Natural Meditative State
- Practice—Body Scan Meditation Exercise
- Practice—Defining Your Space Exercise: Who Am I?
- Case Study—Maria Defining Her Space
- Practice—Safe Space Guided Meditation Exercise
- The Body and the Unconscious
- Practice—Body Tune-In Exercise

WHAT IS A NATURAL MEDITATIVE STATE?

Remember, a *meditative state* or alpha state is a nat focused, calm awareness that all people, including you access for their benefit.

Everyone experiences a light alpha state from time t they are not aware of it at the time or didn't know wha state was. For example, you may go into a trance-like r the highway when you are driving a long distance, espe driving at a consistent speed. Or you may arrive at work ber much about the journey there because you were Your unconscious mind got you to work, but your cor in a relaxed, automatic state. This state is a form of use the terms "alpha state" and "meditative state" int

It's easy to harness this power of the mind. Once meditative state, you can give yourself positive rein use alpha state with certain imagery to walk yoursel ple, stressful work or relationship situations and sce self-assured way. By instilling a sense of calmness are setting the stage for more positive results in y and getting closer to your goals. You are progran and unconscious mind to work together to natur he people and actions that are necessary to ach

PRACTICE—
BODY SCAN MEDITATION EXERCISE

This exercise is called the Body Scan meditation exercise. This exercise is one way to induce alpha state or a meditative state. You will need at least 10–15 minutes without interruptions to practice this exercise.

NOTE: You may find it helpful to slowly read the following script a few times to get used to it, and then read it into an audio recorder to play back for yourself as you stay in a relaxed position. However, you can still learn to reach a relaxed meditative state if you choose to participate with your eyes open (or closed) without recording the script.

To Begin

Get as comfortable as you can in your chair with both feet flat on the ground. Take a moment now to close your eyes and make sure you are comfortable.

Now, begin to mentally scan your body: start with the very top of your head, through your forehead and neck, progressing slowly all the way down through each part of your body at your own pace, visiting each part of the body, even down to the soles of your feet. As you bring awareness down into every area of your body, notice any place that you may hold stress or tension (pause)... |Just notice them for now, recognize these spots, and then move on, continuing to slowly scan your whole body, becoming curious about what your body feels like (pause)...

Allow yourself to take some relaxed, open belly breaths, letting the air fill your lungs and press into the belly ... feeling the rise and fall of your belly (pause)... Now imagine that your breath goes to one of the tight or tense areas... Notice as the breath goes there ... the area begins to loosen and relax. Loosening ... relaxing... Again, breathe gently into that area ... feeling relaxed ... breathing gently ... loosening ... and relaxing ... loosening and relaxing even more… You may choose to bring the breath to another part of the body and that new area begins to loosen and relax (pause)…

Take a moment to notice the thoughts in your head. Just notice what's there right now … you don't have to do anything with them or to them… Notice… What are you thinking right now?… Do you see the thoughts float in front of your mind's eye?… Where do you sense the thoughts?… Where do they reside in your body?… Breathe gently and just be curious (pause)…

Let the thoughts turn into clouds … floating … in the blue sky … of your mind's eye. Allow the thoughts to just float by you … each thought turning into a white, fluffy cloud… Watch them float by you for a moment… Notice each thought in your mind transform easily … and let it float by (pause)… Observe and let them go with each breath… Notice you may feel like a neutral observer… Watching… Unattached… Watching the clouds disappear into the horizon … smaller … with each moment… The blue sky becomes clearer and clearer … the clouds floating away … disappearing… Breathing gently (pause)…

Imagine that the blue sky becomes you … becomes your whole body… Notice your whole body … from your head down to your toes … as you inhale … allowing this calming, radiant blue sky to fill your whole body and mind for a moment, completely clear… Completely calm… Completely at ease in the clarity… Enlarge the blue sky just a bit and let it fill you even more… Relaxing into your breath…

Notice that the calmness and clarity helps you … helps you to naturally access any tools … any information you need now in your daily life… As you take another gentle breath, notice you are more calm, more relaxed, more at ease (pause)…

When you are ready, open your eyes, bring yourself back into the room, stretch and notice that you feel more relaxed, yet recharged. And, in this way, you may move into the next phase of your day.

Action Step

Practice this exercise at least twice this week (or more if you'd like). Notice one change in your life and write about it. One change I have noticed:

PRACTICE—
DEFINING YOUR SPACE EXERCISE:
WHO AM I?

Now that you are learning that a meditative state can be an easy, natural way of being, we are going to learn a basic tool called "defining your space."

Defining your space is, in a nutshell, creating space for the concept of "you"—I call this space your "personal circle." This includes cleaning old beliefs and thoughts out of your space that you may have picked up from others and no longer serve your higher life vision. In later chapters, you will learn how to even keep old, unhelpful societal beliefs out of your space. This defining your space activity helps you keep true to yourself, while keeping any negative or unhelpful beliefs from both the collective and from those around you in your life.

Part One

This is your personal circle. Imagine this circle represents who you are as a whole, complete person. The black dot with the word "Me" in it is your core self. This is you when you are centered and calm, at your

— 35 —

true state. This is what you look like when you're not taking in anybody else's energy or "stuff"—none of their thoughts, beliefs, or feelings as a substitute for yours. The larger circle around the "Me" represents that restful, centered feeling when you have a strong line to keep outside forces from creeping in and you are clear with your boundaries. When you're in this centered state, you know who you are and you can clean out other people's unhealthy, negative, unhelpful thoughts, beliefs, or judgments.

This centered part of you is always within. That part of you is timeless and knows what you want and value. It knows what you came here to be and to achieve as a woman. I am here to cheer you on and hold space for you to be happy and healthy and complete—whatever that means to your core.

To get your unconscious to remember that state of a defined you, drawing this space helps to activate that state, as easy as it sounds. So, in the following exercise, I invite you to take a pen or pencil (it can be any color you choose) and draw a circle around the black dot.

Step 1. Write the word "me" inside the black dot while saying, "This is my space for me."

Step 2. Draw your personal circle around the black dot while saying, "I am safe now to define my space and boundaries."

Step 3. Just gaze at your personal circle for a minute or for however long you feel so inclined.

Step 4. Imagine … what do you want from your life?

Step 5. Write it here:

Be as imaginative as you'd like. Start with the first thing that pops into your mind and list a few bullet points:

-
-
-
-
-

Step 6. Go back to your personal circle.

Imagine you're standing in the black dot surrounded by the white space. How does that white space feel? Just notice the feeling in your body—you do not have to write it down.

When Your Boundaries Get Bumped, Broken, or Invaded

Sometimes, people upset us, say something hurtful or judgmental, or tell us their way is better. When that occurs, it may feel like a boundary violation—how does this affect your circle?

When there's a boundary violation, it can seem as though it penetrates or puts holes in our circle. We can all feel this at some point. Part of the human experience is being challenged to grow and transform. This includes learning how to navigate the interpersonal web of relationships and develop the mental muscle to keep your circle "intact" when someone tries to bump, break, or invade it.

It is a normal part of every person's growth process to learn to strengthen our personal circle and make it impervious to the judgments (or even the good intentions) of others. For example, sometimes our loved ones may think they know better than us what would be good for us. Their advice and comments mean well but can still be boundary violations. Most of the time, their advice and comments stem from their commitment to follow some of unspoken rules that might exist within your family or community. They are not necessarily malicious in intent—but they are still boundary violations because they are unconsciously intended to stop us from progressing, changing, or growing. When people are unconsciously committed to these rules, they can feel threatened or fearful when you go against the status quo so they will unintentionally try to block you or stop you.

This is how I symbolize that bumped feeling in a person's boundary circle (shown on next page).

Sometimes boundary violations can come directly from society's unspoken "rules" that we feel we need to abide by—this can happen when it feels like other people's expectations define us, rather than our own values and desires.

Some examples of these unspoken "rules" in society include the following.

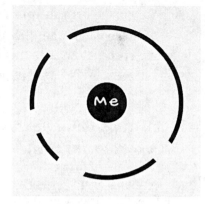

- You should be nice.

- Girls should be polite.

- Women should behave.

- Women should be humble.

- Women shouldn't be provocative.

- Women should be available all the time.

- Women should take care of other people before themselves.

Some people might argue that some of these unspoken "rules" served a purpose at one time. But they have become embedded in some societies in a way that is unproductive and harmful and does not promote circumstances that allow people to thrive.

This isn't to say that all unspoken "rules" are bad. Some unspoken "rules" might actually be helpful, like the Golden Rule that reminds us to treat others how we would like to be treated.

The point here is that societal rules are not a black and white "rules are bad" thing. Some rules help us; for example, "You should stop at a red light." This is a helpful rule—it promotes efficiency and safety. If I ran a red light, I would probably be badly injured. I think that some unspoken societal beliefs probably developed out of a need, just like "People should stop at a red light." Have you seen what happens at an intersection if there is not a light? It tends to take more time to figure out whose turn it is to cross. You are not bound by a red light rule, but you then need to think through whose turn it is to go, and this usually takes more conscious thought and time.

At this point, just start being aware of when your boundaries are being bumped, whether by well-meaning friends or society's unspoken "rules." By tuning in to when that happens, you'll bring your unconscious information into your conscious awareness and have a better understanding of why that violated your boundary. Through this process of human growth, you'll be able to pull your unconscious beliefs up and ask, "Is this belief helpful to me or not?" That's part of building your mental muscle. I'm not saying throw out all the beliefs you've learned from the collective—I'm saying to learn how to personally choose which beliefs are helpful to you and which ones aren't, so that the ones that aren't don't get in your way.

So the point of this exercise is to tune in to who you are as a balanced whole person and think about how you want to relate to others. What are values you've learned from mentors that work for you and you make your own? What are some optional rules that you blindly, unconsciously swallowed from the collective culture that do not help you either personally or in your relations with others? There are probably thousands of beliefs we have collected from our interactions with the world and I would bet most of them are helpful. This exercise is really just helping you be aware of how you would like to consciously examine some previously unconsciously held beliefs that may have hindered you in the past. Remember the phone analogy—some apps are helpful, and some are old apps that you can delete, some are old apps that you can upgrade to new, more helpful belief apps.

This is some deep stuff that we're talking about. Take a moment to stand up and stretch ... raise your hands up, shake your arms and your legs, feel your muscles lengthening and the blood flowing again.

Part Two

After you take some time to stretch, notice the diagram below with the broken lines that represent when your circle feels violated. Write on each blank line the phrase "Other people's beliefs." This activity is simply telling your subconscious mind that you are recognizing that other people's information has gotten in your space when you feel your boundaries

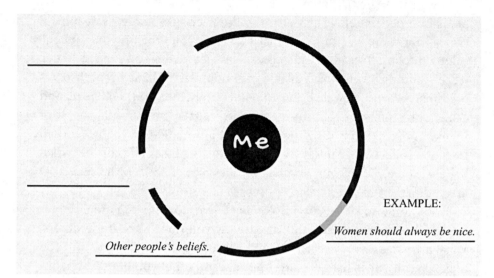

EXAMPLE:

Women should always be nice.

Other people's beliefs.

have been violated. You can write the phrase "Other people's beliefs" on each blank line. Or, if you want to challenge yourself, you can write down a specific belief from others you feel violated your personal circle. In the example above, I wrote the phrase "Women should always be nice." Then, fill in the blank space in the circle with a line as shown above. By filling in the circle, you are telling your subconscious to kick that belief out of your mental space. Got it?

CASE STUDY—
MARIA DEFINING HER SPACE

Maria came to work with me because she felt tired and drained all the time as well as unhappy with her current work. She had a decent job as a bookkeeper and it paid fine, but she wanted something else. She felt like something was missing but she wasn't sure what. Maria lived with her boyfriend, but she wasn't sure they were on the same page. She wanted more stability. They tended to move more than she wanted and she wanted to be in a home where they stayed for more than a year or two. She was 41 and had a 10-year-old from her previous marriage. She and her ex-husband shared custody. Her boyfriend was very kind to her child; he thrived on adventure, though, and didn't like any boredom. Her ex-husband was also a "good man" and the traditional provider. She married him because she felt it was that time of life and they got along well and her family really approved of him. After several years, she felt stale and they amicably parted ways. She said that she felt it was societal pressure to "get married" originally.

When we worked together doing the Muse process, Maria and I started exploring "who got in her space." In her coaching, she seemed scattered because she let other people's ideas of what she should be in her space—their opinions crept in on her thoughts and decisions. For example, when we first explored new ideas for what she wanted in her career, she said she wanted to go back to school to become a physician's assistant. She liked science and helping people.

As we co-created action steps, she received an offer to help manage a medical office, which paid more than her current job, and she could explore what physician assistants did in their daily work activities. Then she could decide if that was the career path for her. However, she was lethargic about following through—even though she seemed so enthusiastic in coaching about the initial idea of being a physician's assistant.

When someone says one thing and does another that is an important clue that she is being pulled by some unconscious beliefs that conflict with her true self. She could be acting on an unconscious voice from society telling her, "This is what you should be," or trying to please someone she is close to who might have said something like, "You would really be good at medical assisting." If she is lethargic on following through with one of her goals, I know she has someone else's voice in her circle, so to speak.

I had Maria do this exercise (on following page).

2. Relaxed Alpha State = Meditative State

Part One

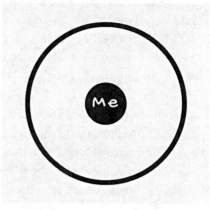

This is your personal circle. Imagine this circle represents who you are as a whole, complete person. The black dot with the word "Me" in it is your core self. This is you when you are centered and calm, at your true state. This is what you look like when you're not taking in anybody else's energy or "stuff"—none of their thoughts, beliefs or feelings as a substitute for yours. The larger circle around the "Me" represents that restful, centered feeling when you have a strong line to keep outside forces from creeping in and you are clear with your boundaries. When you're in this centered state, you know who you are and you can clean out other people's unhealthy, negative, unhelpful thoughts, beliefs, or judgments.

This centered part of you is always within. That part of you is timeless and knows what you want and value. It knows what you came here to be and to achieve as a woman. I am here to cheer you on and hold space for you to be happy and healthy and complete—whatever that means to your core.

To get your unconscious to remember that state of a defined you, drawing this space helps to activate that state, as easy as it sounds. So, in the following exercise, I invite you to take a pen or pencil (it can be any color you choose) and draw a circle around the black dot.

Step 1. Write the word "me" inside the black dot while saying, "This is my space for me."

Step 2. Draw your personal circle around the black dot (see following page) while saying, "I am safe now to define my space and boundaries."

Step 3. Just gaze at the image for a minute or for however long you feel so inclined.

Step 4. Imagine … what do you want from your life?

Step 5. Write it here:

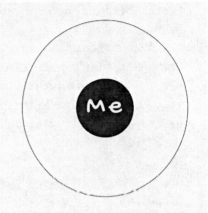

Be as imaginative as you'd like.

Start with the first thing that pops into your mind and list a few bullet points:

- *To be happy*
- *To have fulfilling work*
- *To have a close partnership*
- *To be close with my child*

Step 6. Go back to the circle drawing.

Imagine you're standing in the black dot surrounded by the white space. How does that white space feel? *Calm.*

Part Two

In our follow-up sessions, Maria and I explored action steps to further her along the path to her goals. For instance, one goal we discussed was for her to set up an appointment to visit the medical office. When Maria didn't follow through with that, I knew some unconscious beliefs were getting in her way. To figure out what those beliefs were, we drew the dotted circle and explored what subconscious beliefs were getting in the way.

We just became curious about what those beliefs may have been. She used the Body Scan exercise from the beginning of this chapter to help her get into a more relaxed state, where she was able to just observe what thoughts came to her mind. After the Body Scan exercise, we looked at her circle again and she wrote down the following.

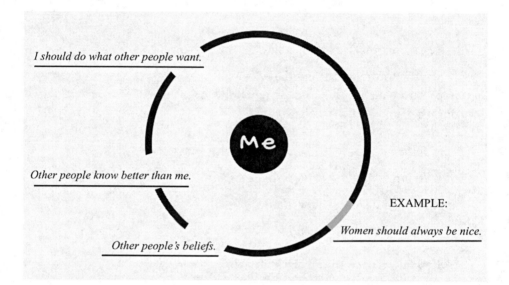

I should do what other people want.

Me

Other people know better than me.

EXAMPLE:

Women should always be nice.

Other people's beliefs.

We did this exercise a few times over the next few sessions, and Maria realized that her subconscious mind held the beliefs "Other people know better than me" and "I should do what other people want." This helped her realize that the position at the medical office was aligned with what other people wanted for her—not what she wanted for herself. She was lethargic about this new opportunity because it was not aligned with her desires, but she did not realize that until she did this exercise and was able to see that she was trying to mold herself to match other people's expectations. The procrastination was her subconscious trying to tell her this was not the right opportunity for her.

A few weeks later, Maria was offered a new position that she was much more enthusiastic about. This was a bookkeeping job with a company that had a training program in their human resources (HR) department. In the job offer, the company told her that she could eventually join the training program and be paid to develop HR skills. Maria was much more excited about this opportunity and accepted the position without hesitation. She thrived in the HR training program and eventually became a director of human resources.

She followed up with these exercises of defining her space whenever she felt self-doubt and needed to reconnect with her values and voice.

REVISITING
YOUR LIFE VISION

Now that you have had some practice defining your space more clearly, let's revisit your life vision.

Your life vision just becomes you, like breathing, once you define your space on a regular basis. Think of defining your space like brushing your teeth. Go back to the Life Vision exercise from Chapter 1—write down your life vision here.

My life vision is…

Now we're going to discuss and practice another technique to help you go into this helpful alpha state. This next exercise will incorporate your life vision in a new way and help it get coded into your unconscious mind.

PRACTICE—
SAFE PLACE GUIDED
MEDITATION EXERCISE

Earlier you learned that the brain produces a certain wavelength called alpha brainwaves and this produces a meditative, calm state in you. As with learning to ride a bicycle or drive a car, a little practice can go a long way. Let's practice a meditation. I call this Safe Place Guided Meditation exercise.

This exercise is one way to induce alpha state or a meditative state. You will need at least 10–15 minutes without interruptions to practice this exercise.

NOTE: You may find it helpful to slowly read the following script a few times to get used to it, and then read it into an audio recorder to play back for yourself as you stay in a relaxed position. However, you can still learn to reach a relaxed meditative state if you choose to participate with your eyes open (or closed) without recording the script.

To begin this guided meditation, I invite you to sit or lie down in a comfortable position and close your eyes. Kindly notice your body and be aware of any tension. As you exhale, notice the tension leaving your body as your breath flows out. Allow your breathing to gradually slow down at your own pace... Just tuning into the breath for however long feels good to you...

As you do this, allow yourself to picture in your mind a safe place. Notice what first comes to mind. What type of place does your mind choose as a safe place...?

Some people choose a natural setting, like a beach or meadow. If it's a beach, what do the waves look like? What do they sound like? Some people may feel the mist on their face, taste the salt on their tongue... Allow yourself to notice if there any birds overhead. You may hear the sound of the birds chirping, singing a song. Notice if there are any breezes in this place, feel the wind on your cheeks...

Notice the ground beneath your feet. Is it dirt or sand, or maybe something else? What does it feel like on your feet? Just know that whatever you experience here is just right for you...

Allow yourself to lie down in the safe place and feel the ground beneath your body. Notice the gentle ground below warming your body, allowing you to relax even more and feel safe and comfortable during this meditation. Feel the weight of your body resting on the ground allowing gravity to help you release any tension into the ground and let go of it. Imagine that with each breath you breathe that any tension gets washed away with the breath... Look above you into this sky and notice the color of the sky. Is the sun shining? Is the sky clear? Notice if there any trees around. What kind of leaves do they have? What color are the leaves? Pick one of the leaves and notice what it feels like, what its texture is like.

Notice a tree stump in this place. If you feel like it, go and sit on this stump, feeling the sun above your head warming you and further relaxing you. Breathe in the warmth and vibrancy of the sun, allowing it to fill you with a sense of calm and peace from the top of your head to the tips of your toes. As you become part of your safe place, notice that you feel more rested, more relaxed, more at peace... When you're ready, allow yourself to come back into this room and leave your safe place for now, knowing that at any time you can return to your safe place, anytime you need... After you have thoroughly connected with this place, open your eyes. In the same relaxed position, continue to breathe smoothly and rhythmically and take a few moments to experience and enjoy your relaxing guided meditation. Your safe place is available to you whenever you need to go there.

If you would like a short audio version of this to listen to, visit my website at www.drbarbaracox.com.

2. Relaxed Alpha State = Meditative State

In this relaxed state, again notice your life vision:

What is your life vision now? Is it different from before the exercise? Is it the same vision, but maybe clearer and more vibrant?

My life vision is...

What does it feel like to write down your life vision after completing the safe place meditation? This exercise is helping you to feel that it is now safe to have a happy and fulfilled life, including enjoyable work, family, and friends.

After doing this set of exercises, Maria began to attract a few new friends with interests more aligned with hers. In addition, her boyfriend even decided after they communicated their personal goals and visions that he was happy to remain in the town they were currently in. Over that year, they also began discussing having a child together. They realized that they were at the tail end of childbearing years. They both were interested in having a child, as they had seen their own relationship and careers blossom.

THE BODY
AND THE UNCONSCIOUS

Now that you are clear on your life vision, we want to clear out any barriers or unconscious patterns that could inhibit your vision from becoming a reality. Remember that the body stores many of your unconscious patterns. That also means the body plays a pivotal role in shifting those patterns. When you tune in to your body, you engage different parts of your body to generate a shift in your unconscious patterns. This is a concept that makes the work in this book unique in that we're engaging both the mind and the body. You do not even need to be consciously aware that the shift is happening.

Let's use a hypothetical example so you know how this works. Since your unconscious holds reflexes that help keep you safe, the following exercise and discussion will help reassure your unconscious mind that you are currently safe.

Let's say, for example, that your body holds the memory of your parent disciplining you in your left arm. Maybe you were angry and you yelled at her, so she grabbed your left arm and yanked you out of the store. She may have been well meaning in trying to diffuse the situation and teach you that there's a better way to express your anger than having a tantrum in the middle of the grocery store. However, your subconscious stored that as a reflex—that anytime you express your anger, you are going to be grabbed on your left arm. It was really trying to protect you. You instinctively and unconsciously tense your left arm and prepare yourself to be punished or disciplined when you express your anger. This is not to say we blame our parents for disciplining us; this is an example to show that sometimes, our instinctive subconscious mind makes overarching generalizations from one specific experience. This exercise will help your body let go of some of the overarching generalizations that it has held on to from the past and be more receptive to new ways of relating.

PRACTICE— BODY TUNE-IN EXERCISE

Here is an exercise that will tune you in to your body and help you prepare to shift unconscious patterns. We'll revisit this exercise again in later parts of the book to engage the body more actively prior to doing some of the future exercises. After you've practiced this exercise a few times and gotten comfortable with it, it won't take you long to do it and quickly tune in to your body.

Take a deep breath ... inhale ... and pause for a beat at the top ... now exhale through the mouth, pausing for a beat at the bottom... Do that one more time slowly ... inhale ... and pause for a beat at the top... Now exhale through the mouth, pausing for a beat at the bottom. And one more big deep breath ... inhale ... and pause for a beat at the top... Now exhale through the mouth, pausing for a beat at the bottom. And as you continue, make the exhale a little longer than the inhale...

Continue with these deep breaths, and tune in to your tailbone. Feel the chair holding you, making contact with your muscles. Gently move your tailbone back and forth, feeling that space ground you and center you...

Continue your deep breaths, and move your focus up to your body center, right inside your belly ... feel the muscles in your core contract for a moment ... focus on the strength that it gives your entire body...

As you continue your deep breaths, work your way up toward your rib cage, focus on your solar plexus, which is the spot right between your ribs ... feel it engage while you inhale and exhale ... feel how it helps your breath flow through your body...

And continue to take more deep breaths while you shift your focus to your heart ... concentrate on the lightness you feel deep in your chest ... notice how it rises and falls with every inhale and exhale...

And as you take another deep breath, move your focus to your throat ... sense how the energy in your throat expands as you connect to it ... sense how any blocks you might feel in your communication start to dissipate ... feel the channels of communication start to open and notice your internal voice strengthening...

Continue your deep breaths and now shift your focus up to the spot on your forehead right between your eyes ... feel a lightness fill your body when you focus here ... feel how it clears your mind, relaxes your jaw, and softens your shoulders...

Now take another deep breath and tune in to the point just above your head... Feel a positive current run through your body, a gold-like energy running up and down ... sense how your body lifts and expands, and notice how you stand taller and stretch your spine to touch that point...

Take one more deep breath and imagine yourself connected to all seven points at the same time ... inhale ... and pause for a beat at the top... Now exhale through the mouth, pausing for a beat at the bottom. You are now tuned in to your body. You may even feel lighter and more energized.

Isn't it great to be in alpha state and to be connected to your body? The more you do these exercises, the more aware you will be of your body and more easily identify what you need and feel.

This chapter teaches you that the easiest path to reach your life goals is to define your life vision, then access your natural meditative alpha state to help you define your space and be aware of any bumps or violations that might be occurring. Your meditative alpha state helps you access those parts of you that are in tune with a higher purpose for your life, the part that has your best interests and happiness in line. Now that we've learned these tools, we can move on to see how they help you connect with your intuition.

....

KEY TAKE-AWAYS

✓ The first key for this chapter of the book: *understand that meditation is a natural state of focused, calm awareness that all people can access for their benefit.*

2. Relaxed Alpha State = Meditative State

✓ The second key for this chapter of the book: *understand what it means to define your space and practice the Defining Your Space exercise a few times.*

✓ The third key for this chapter of the book: *realize that the body stores unconscious patterns and connecting to your body helps shift those patterns.*

CHAPTER 3

Following Your Intuition

"Life isn't something you can give an answer to today. You should enjoy the process of waiting, the process of becoming what you are. There is nothing more delightful than planting flower seeds and not knowing what kind of flowers are going to come up."—Milton H. Erickson

This chapter will introduce you to the concept of intuition and how to access it. Following your intuition and gut hunches can be easy to learn, and you can also choose to practice it to get even better at it. One easy way to get there is by meditation. Meditation is simply *the act of focusing your attention on one thing for a period of time.* It is a natural state of calm, focused awareness that you can use toward a beneficial goal. This chapter will help you reinforce the natural meditative state (called an alpha state) that you learned in the previous chapter and will show you how to change any conscious and unconscious programming that may hold you back. This applies not only at work, but also in other areas of your life like friendships, relationships, and finances. It also will teach you to validate your intuitive hunches, helping you learn to trust your gut. I invite you to use your intuition more often in everyday decision-making activities. Trust me; you will learn very specific, fun, and easy exercises that you can start applying right away.

Here is the roadmap showing what you will learn in Chapter 3.

- What Leads to an Intuitive State?
- Learning to Follow Your Gut More Often
- Dealing with Resistance
- What Does Work Bring?

- What Does Life Bring?
- Unwrap Your Gifts
- What to Do If Things Feel Vague

WHAT LEADS TO
AN INTUITIVE STATE?

When we go into a focused state, it leads to alpha brain wave patterns. These brain wave patterns heighten intuition and intuitive states. Accessing your intuition can be easy to learn, and you can practice it over time to get better at it. One easy way to get there is by meditation, which leads to the alpha state (which we discussed in the prior chapter). Meditation is basically the act of focusing your attention on one thing for a period of time. It doesn't have to be woo-woo or complicated. It is a natural state of calm, focused awareness that you can use toward a beneficial goal. In fact, there are probably times when you've fallen into a natural meditative state and didn't even realize it (like when you're "in the zone" on a run or when you get to your destination and don't remember the drive at all).

Many scientists have studied meditation over the years to determine the "active ingredients" for how it works. One mind-body research group studied meditators of various backgrounds. It found that anyone could achieve this focused, alpha state by meditating,[1] regardless of his or her background, religion, or belief system. That's because it is a natural in-born state of mind that anyone can access, including you. The research also found that meditation can be learned in a few simple steps. Meditation has been shown to have lasting health effects as well and can foster a sense of well-being. Learning this tool will not only help you reach your work-life goal via increased intuition, but also provide many great additional benefits.

Before we do any exercises, let's break down meditation into a few simple steps. There are two basic steps to all forms of meditation.[2] I add a third step for our purposes of work-life balance in the Muse Process meditations. (After you read this and you then practice these steps, it is helpful to close your eyes and be in a relatively quiet place.)

Step 1. Keep your repeated focus on something—a word, an object, a sound. You can simply focus on your **breath**, as you did in Chapter 1.

Step 2. Gently release everyday thoughts that cross your mind and continue focusing on the word, the object, the sound, or your breath.

Step 3. Ask your very creative unconscious for a novel solution to one problem you'd like to resolve. See, feel, or sense what arises.

I encourage you to practice these steps a few times a day until you get comfortable doing them. When you're just starting to learn how to meditate, you might feel like you're not "doing it right." But that's not true. If you just follow the steps above for three minutes or five minutes or 15 minutes (or however long you want to do it for), that's meditating! It's normal to have your mind drift and wander, to lose your focus on the word and start thinking about your grocery list or what you have to do next … when that happens, notice that your mind has wandered and gently bring it back to your focus word. Don't be hard on yourself when this occurs—it's part of the meditation process.

LEARNING TO FOLLOW YOUR GUT MORE OFTEN

Both for myself and with my clients, I have found that having a specific amount of time to go within and meditate daily helps one to get in tune with what the inner self really wants. The more we are barraged with external stimuli from electronic devices, our phones, the TV, the more we overwhelm our inner guidance system. People that take time to decompress and tune in to their inner voice by going someplace quiet for a few minutes a day tend to get very insightful gut hunches that lead them down the most optimal life path with ease.

As a mom and a business owner, I know how hard it can be to find a spare 20 minutes to do an "official" daily meditation to access my intuition. Here's the good news: meditation doesn't have to be difficult or time-consuming. You can actually meditate without giving it much thought. Achieving a meditative state can happen during many activities that you do often, things like

- washing the dishes;
- mowing the lawn
- going for a long walk or run;
- driving home from work;
- using the elliptical machine or treadmill; and
- sweeping the driveway.

Really, any repetitive behavior that lulls you into a rhythmic activity works. By focusing on the task itself—what your body's doing, what your breath is like, how your muscles feel—these simple activities put you in a meditative state. All of these things (and many more I will show you) are meditative activities you can use for your benefit. Next time you do the chores on your to-do list, use the opportunity to help yourself gain more clarity and intuitive insights. Anything repetitive that helps turn off the analytic brain for a bit and let it rest helps to open up that vast storehouse of information in the intuitive brain.

When you are making a decision and feel stuck it is also helpful to access your intuitive mind by tuning in to your feelings. Instead of over-thinking a decision, ask "How do I feel in my body if I do Choice A or Choice B?" The more you practice this tuning in to what the body wants, the easier things flow. You can also follow gut feelings when meeting a potential friend, co-worker or mate. When I meet someone new, I always go within and ask myself, "How do I feel in my body when I am around this person at this moment?" Notice the first feeling that arises. Not the analytic mind's chatter of how others say you should feel, but how you actually feel at that moment in the person's presence.

People can improve their intuition over time by practice—just like building a muscle. What does "practicing" look like? Well, it is all about learning to be more accepting of gut hunches and using the unconscious information that flashes into our awareness spontaneously. You can get in touch with that storehouse of information you hold in your unconscious by learning to follow your gut hunches. When people access their intuition and pay attention to their hunches, they tend to make better decisions.

Furthermore, workplaces are more and more often seeing the value of the traditionally held concept of "women's intuition," which allows us to collect data en masse and identify patterns in the data.[3] Essentially, our intuition helps us take stock of what is happening in our overall environment and make meaning of that data. It alerts us to know when something is off and when something new is on the horizon. These flashes of insight that alert us to changes are thought to arise from the right side of the brain, which is holistic and intuitive. These insights usually arise spontaneously, without us having to go through the slower, analysis system of our left brain. Use this flow toward integration by accepting both the left and right brain presentation of data to your advantage. Use those visceral feelings you get in your gut to assess all the opportunities that are out there for you. You do not have to rely only on analysis and conscious thought to make a choice. Connect with your body and its holistic wisdom too. Connect with your innate sense of intuition.

One easy activity to practice connecting with your gut hunches is to choose between two restaurant choices solely by using your intuition. Look at the menu of one restaurant and ask your gut, "How does this feel to me?" Then ask your gut the same of the other restaurant. Choose the one that your gut hunch says that you will enjoy the most. With this simple type of trusting your gut activity, you will begin to build up your intuitive muscle.

If you have trouble tuning in to your gut hunches, that's okay. You may have ignored your intuition's voice so often that over time, you may have developed a barrier to hearing or feeling it. In the next few pages, you can teach yourself to dismantle any barriers or blocks to your inner voice by allowing those blocks—the fearful part of us—to speak first. Ready?

DEALING WITH RESISTANCE

In Chapter 1, you described in detail your ideal life vision. It's easier to create it in real life when you have a concrete vision of what gives you joy. If any part of you resists having what you want for whatever reason or something says, "You can't have that for such and such reason," ask that resistant part, "What do you need to feel safe as this goal completes?"

Take a relaxed breath and listen to what it tells you—it may just give you a sensation. Promise you will keep it safe. Then, do this exercise—close your eyes, take a relaxed full breath and exhale, then say, "The more I resist this life goal, the easier it happens. Oh well."

Have that "resistant" part of you now write out your ideal life vision scenario again below. In addition, ask it to add in any extra life details it needs to feel safe as it completes your life vision.

My life vision feels safe to complete when…

Most of us have a part of us that resists change, even helpful, happy change—I'll call that part our "fearful self." This is the part that wants to keep us safe at all costs. Some people's fearful self is so over-developed that it has them hide out from life—it is the part that says, "Always stay home, don't take any risks."

Most people keep their fearful self in balance, luckily. They just have it speak up when they are doing something that may really be physically dangerous, say, skydiving, for example. It just checks in to see that all the other parts of you are in tune with doing that activity. Let's say you are curious to learn skydiving, but you are not very athletic. The fearful voice may have you check the statistics on the safety of skydiving and what you need to do to be prepared physically. That is one way it keeps you safe but not hidden from the adventures of life.

Ask that resistant part of you (while you are imagining that your life vision has already happened), "When this life vision scenario happened, what were you afraid of? What were you trying to protect me from?"

Write its answer below.

In order to help that part of you feel even safer, please answer the following questions:

How will you reassure that fearful part of you as you finish your life goal?

How will you remind that part of you that you will protect yourself?

Just checking in with that fearful self and reminding it that you will do safety checks every so often can help it to settle down. Also, doing any of the meditations included in this book can give it a sense of security and calm.

Let's revisit the vision you created in the Chapter 1 exercise Envision Your Ideal Work-Life Situation, where you described in detail your ideal situation, in essence, your work-life goal. Now we are going to ask our resistant self to support us in this vision. Check in with your intuition and ask yourself how that goal feels now. Does it still feel right? Does it need a little tweaking?

If your life vision is the same, write it here below. If it needs a little tweaking, change it up a bit and write your new one below. Let your gut and your intuition guide you:

All parts of me support my life vision now, which is...

WHAT DOES WORK BRING?

Now that we've started calming down the fearful part of brain, we can start accessing the creative abilities and insights of the right brain—the intuitive part of the brain. The following exercise helps to unlock it and let it flow as it relates to your work, job, and career.

Part One

One way that we can get in touch with our intuitive mind is to do an exercise that is based on a psychology technique of word association. The following exercise is a way to access the hidden parts of your mind. Get a piece of blank paper and write the phrase "Work brings _____." Write this phrase 20 times on your piece of paper (include the blank line exactly as written).

Then, take a minute to fill in the blanks with the first words that pop into your mind to complete the phrase "Work brings..." Do it quickly, without thinking about it. The words do not have to make sense to you. (I recommend setting a timer for 60 seconds to help you to do this quickly.)

This exercise helps clear out the subconscious mind and makes you more aware of possible subconscious patterns you have about your work or business. We'll be shifting these patterns with more exercises to come to ensure your success. Even the act of writing the phrase 20 times helps activate various parts of the brain to work together more harmoniously. This exercise also can lead to intuitive insights that help you in moving forward.

Part Two

In the last exercise, What Does Work Bring? Part One, we did an activity to clear out the subconscious mind to make you more aware of possible subconscious patterns have about your work or business.

Now, I invite you to reflect on that exercise below:

- Was there anything that surprised you when you did this exercise?

- What subconscious beliefs about work may be hindering you?

- What subconscious beliefs about work may be helping you?

Note any other awareness or insights you had after doing this exercise:

WHAT DOES LIFE BRING?

We are going to expand on the above writing exercise because it is so powerful. I have researched the power of expressive writing for years and it can help you accomplish amazing things. Instead of just focusing on work-related issues, now we are going to ask the right brain to expand on the topic to include life in general. Let's be curious and see what happens.

3. Following Your Intuition

Part One

On another piece of paper, write the phrase "Life brings _____" 20 times. Then, take a minute to write down the first words that pop into your mind that complete the phrase "Life brings..." Do it quickly, without thinking about it. The words do not have to make sense to you. (I recommend setting a timer for 60 seconds to help you to do this quickly.)

As noted previously, this exercise helps clear out the subconscious mind and makes you more aware of possible subconscious patterns you have about your life in general. Some clients even notice positive and helpful patterns they have regarding life after doing this exercise.

Part Two

In the last exercise, What Does Life Bring? Part One, we did an activity to clear out the subconscious mind to make you more aware of possible subconscious patterns have about your life in general.

Now, I invite you to reflect on that exercise below:

- Was there anything that surprised you when you did this exercise?

- What subconscious beliefs about life may be hindering you?

- What subconscious beliefs about life may be helping you?

Note any other awareness or insights you had after doing this exercise:

Now, we are really going to get rolling and let our intuition flow. In this book, you are learning a series of organized exercises to grow and strengthen your intuition—just like a seed growing into a flower.

After a while, intuition will just seem normal to you, like breathing. After all, you don't have to do structured exercises to breathe; a part of you just knows how to breathe. You are connecting with that part.

UNWRAP YOUR GIFTS

This exercise is one way to access subconscious "gifts" you may have presently and may not have been aware of previously. Happiness researchers have shown that regularly counting our current blessings and gifts actually boosts our level of contentment. To create a positive goal in our life most easily, we need to feel content and full now. We can create anything we want, even when stressed or unhappy. However, we can reach goals more quickly when we aren't dragged down by negativity.

Imagine, feel, see, hear, or in some way sense that you are in front of a movie screen and on that screen appears five presents wrapped in beautiful, crisp wrapping paper with large sparkly bows on each present. Imagine that you can now step into that movie screen and be surrounded by those five presents; they may even multiply as you become part of that movie. Be curious. Look around and grab one of the presents. Begin opening the present. Notice any sensations that come to you as you open that present. Is the paper green or some other color? Is the paper crinkly or smooth? How many bows are on the present? Are there other decorations on the present? What smells are associated with unwrapping it? What do you notice about the process of unwrapping the gift? What is the gift?

Describe the gift:

Finish unwrapping the other four gifts and note what they are:

Gift #2:

Gift #3:

Gift #4:

Gift #5:

The next exercise is an additional way to tune in to your intuitive self. This exercise can give us messages in ways other than analytic reasoning.

WHAT TO DO IF THINGS FEEL VAGUE

If you feel that you need new ways to tap into your intuition, especially if you feel unsure or vague, here is another way. The best way for you to learn this is to follow along with a case example.

The CEO and founder of a skin care line came to work with me in order to make her current goals more clear and precise. She wanted to launch a product line that was a bit new for her—focusing on moms' and babies' skin care—but her topic was so large it overwhelmed her. She felt scattered and unfocused. She felt disconnected from her intuition.

During our coaching session, she realized she was most excited about the rather large concept goal of helping post-partum women feel sexy and beautiful—to "feel comfortable in their own skin."

Because this was a rather large starting point, we did the following exercise to help her reach a more focused goal. I asked her to think of what made her excited to start a new project or goal. I asked her to pick a specific uplifting feeling that surrounds that goal, for example, excitement, enthusiasm, or enjoyment. I gave her three pieces of paper. Then, she completed the following exercise:

1. Draw a cloud on the first piece of paper and write inside the cloud, "I am feeling fuzzy."

2. Rip up the cloud drawing and throw it away. This symbolizes letting the fuzzy or unclear feeling go.

3. Pick an uplifting feeling: _____. This client picked the feeling "excited."

4. Experience it.

5. While experiencing that uplifting feeling, begin to write about your idea or proposed project on the second piece of paper—that piece of it that most excites you at your core. Write the first thing that pops into your head, let it flow. Do this for a minute or two.

6. On the third piece of paper, draw a circle and write "Target" above it. This symbolizes you having reached your target goal. Ask your intuition what the one most important word or phrase is that pops out from what you wrote on step five. Write that one word or short phrase inside the circle.

After completing the free-form writing, the client told me she had written about using a generic skin care product to lighten stretch marks after the birth of her first child, but she wasn't really happy with the results. She wrote about her background in medical aesthetics, and how, because of that experience, she had decided to mix her own formula. The phrase she put in the circle was "Lighten stretch marks."

As we did this exercise, my client realized that this one product was her current passion and that trying to create other new products to add to her company would dilute her focus. She decided to use that one product as her current target goal. She had another skin care line in several local salons where she knew they would be happy to add an additional product to their display tables.

This seems like a simple, easy technique, but it actually works to organize the subconscious on a deep level. The client left our session with a clear target and a plan, as opposed to when she came in feeling vague and undefined. Use this exercise any time you would like to make a vague idea more defined. It will activate your intuition to bring you a sense of clarity and definition.

Now it is your turn. If you're feeling a little unclear about your next steps, this process can help!

In concluding this chapter on intuition, you have done a variety of exercises and given space to the idea of intuitive gut hunches. Part of accessing your intuition is to just keep things simple. Anytime you feel an intuitive flash or gut hunch just notice it. Stop what you are doing and really tune in. Give space in your life to your intuition and it will serve you well.

KEY TAKE-AWAYS

✓ The first key for this chapter of the book: *just be curious about the next gut hunch you experience this week—notice what a gut hunch feels like.*

✓ The second key for this chapter of the book: *realize you can build your intuition over time with simple activities.*

REFERENCES

1. Benson, H., & Klipper, M.Z. (2000). *The relaxation response.* New York: Morrow.

2. Benson, H., & Klipper, M.Z. (2000). *The relaxation response.* New York: Morrow.

3. Tischler, L. (2017, February 13). *Women's intuition at work.* Retrieved from https://www.fastcompany.com/677933/womens-intuition-work.

Getting Results by Taking Action

"Let your performance do the thinking."—Charlotte Brontë

This chapter is simple but powerful. It will help you commit to doing three to five action steps you generate in this chapter. This chapter also contains a calendar of the next 30 days that you will complete with one action step per day as well as other motivating activities.

These activities are very powerful in that they both motivate you on a conscious, action-oriented mode as well as shift your subconscious from a mode of stagnation to action.

Here is the roadmap showing what you will learn in Chapter 4.

- Practice—The Solution Generator Exercise

- Acknowledge Emotions as You Shift Gears

- Practice—Action Planner Exercise

- Practice—Your Kind Friend

- Practice—Daily Diary of Guided Actions for 30 Days Exercise

PRACTICE—
THE SOLUTION GENERATOR EXERCISE

In the last chapter, we discussed what meditation is and how it helps us access our intuition and creative solutions to get on track to our life vision—our desired goal. It includes these three steps:

Step 1. Keep your repeated focus on something—a word, an object, a sound. You can simply focus on your **breath**, as you did in Chapter 1.

Step 2. Gently release everyday thoughts that cross your mind and continue focusing on the word, the object, the sound, or your breath.

Step 3. Ask your very creative unconscious for a novel solution to one problem you'd like to resolve. See, feel, or sense what arises.

Now let's use this three-step process to help you generate solutions and identify what you will take action on in this chapter. To complete steps 1 and 2, focus on your breath as we did in the Relaxed Breathing Exercise:

Lie comfortably on the floor, place one hand on your upper chest and the other hand on your belly.

For now, breathe how you normally would and notice which hand rises and falls the most.

If you are currently tense or anxious, you tend to breathe from the chest with short, shallow breaths.

If you notice that you are breathing from the chest, begin to move your attention to your belly and notice the weight of your hand there.

Place both hands on your abdomen.

Begin inhaling through your nose, slowly, and imagine that you are completely filling your lungs with air so that the lungs push out your abdomen.

You feel this push on your hands and exhale slowly through your mouth while noticing the movement of the abdomen. Breathe in this manner for a few minutes, inhaling through your nose and exhaling through your mouth, and allow your breathing to relax and slow down even more. To simplify it even more: Just be curious about the air reaching the lowest point of your belly. Do this for however long you wish. A few minutes is just fine. However long you decide is just fine.

Do this for just a few minutes … breathing, tuning in and just noticing the breath.

For Step 3, simply mentally ask your unconscious to show you a few ideas to keep you on track with your life vision. Say, "Self, show me something that would help me with this."

Focus on your breath and don't even notice what arises for a few moments, just notice your breath.

As you are focusing on the breath, write down the first three to five things that pop into your mind to do, even if they don't make sense:

-
-
-
-

Now that you have generated some solution ideas, I invite you to leave what you have written and go do some other activity. For instance, go walk, watch TV, sweep the floor, just anything to release this activity from your awareness for a little while. We will revisit it in the next section of this chapter.

ACKNOWLEDGE EMOTIONS
AS YOU SHIFT GEARS

Sometimes, as we go through the process of shifting unconscious patterns and moving into action steps, we may feel frustration or other emotions. Some people may not experience troubling emotions, but for those who do, let's address this as a potential action step. Just being aware that we can experience emotions, and being open to the experience of a range of emotions, from bliss to anger to anything in between, is helpful to process and release them.

Robert Frost said, "The only way out is through." We often use this saying in reference to difficult times, but it is true for difficult emotions too. Things like anger, sadness, and even envy or frustration are tough emotions to experience. They don't feel pleasant, but they are important.

Let's take anger, for example. Believe it or not, anger has some good points. It is a biological emotion, which means that it exists for a reason—our body system evolved over the eons and anger is part of the operating system. Over the past few years, I've noticed a lot of censoring of anger. I have even noticed people promoting tips and tricks to erase this emotion. The thing is, erasure isn't helpful. These tricks only serve to anesthetize the anger, which actually makes it fester under the surface.

A Warning Signal

What if we thought of anger and other troubling emotions as an alarm signal—to warn us and keep us safe? Our biology evolved our emotional system to protect us. Therefore, we can look at anger as a protective mechanism, not as something bad. We experience anger as a species because there is something to be aware of—something is happening that we should acknowledge. Anger is often responsible for letting us know when our boundaries have been crossed, when our values are at risk, or when we are not being true to ourselves. This warning signal also gives us motivational fuel to change what isn't working. Pay attention to it. Rather than disavowing anger, take time to really look at it. Sit with it (but don't take action) until you really understand what is making you angry.

Here's the thing … anger is not the problem. Sometimes, it's what we do when we are angry that becomes the issue and causes suffering. This is usually due to the lack of coping skills to effectively express and direct the anger.

When we get really angry, we go immediately into "fight or flight" mode. The cortisol and other neurotransmitters get revved up and we're flooded with emotion. We tend to become reactive and aren't often consciously thinking about what we say or do. The challenge is to strengthen your basic coping skills that are built into your system.

Look Before You Leap

Before you take action on your anger, explore the anger first—then you can more effectively express and direct it to a productive outcome. One way to do this is through journaling. The physical and emotional benefits of journaling, as a catharsis of stressful events, have been widely researched by Dr. James Pennebaker[1] as well as by others. According to Pennebaker's research, writing about upsetting feelings or events in our lives can improve physical and mental health. This gives you the energy to move toward your goals.

I often incorporate the journaling research into my work with clients. It is a useful activity for you too in uncovering and processing your anger. The most helpful way to journal is to find a quiet place to write where you will not be disturbed. It also helps to pick a set time of day to schedule the journaling activity. The research recommends writing for a minimum of 15 minutes a day for at least three days. To keep it simple for purposes of the Muse Process, plan on journaling for three days.

4. Getting Results by Taking Action

Once you begin journaling, keep writing in a stream of conscious-ness manner. Write about anything that is bothering you. Do not be concerned about spelling, punctuation or grammar. If you feel like you run out of things to say before the 15 minutes is over, just keep writing. You can even repeat topics or things you wrote about at the beginning. You can write with a pen or pencil or type on the computer. If you are unable to write, you can speak into a voice recorder.

When your journaling is completed, you can do whatever you want to with the written material. I advise my clients to burn it or tear it up. You know I am going to advise you to check in with your intuition. Ask yourself what you feel like doing with the material. The next time you feel an overwhelming sense of anger or frustration, pick up a pen and give it a try. Writing about it for a few days will help you gain a new perspective. You may even gain enough insight to speak your mind and get your needs met.

Anger can be used as fuel to get motivated and change what isn't working in your life for something better. It can help you speak your boundaries and keep them. It can motivate you to ask for better conditions at work—like equal pay and family leave time. It can get you in touch with what you truly value and enjoy in life, rather than just going with another person's idea of what you should do with your life.

Frustration and anger may arise if you feel your progress on your life vision is slow. Believe me, there are times I experienced this. Some-times my plans and dreams would just fall into place and other goals such as the publishing of this book took years. From the time I conceived of this book to the time it took me to get a publisher and get it out to the world took many years. I kept asking myself, "Why is it taking so long?" I was doing everything "right," connecting with published author colleagues, organizing my proposal and beating on the proverbial doors, sending pitch letters, and still nothing had materialized. Getting rejec-tion letters was very draining. I'd read them and feel like throwing in the towel. I was feeling discouraged and a bit defeated. I gave voice to those feelings and simply acknowledged them and kept at my goal. I sometimes wondered what I should do.

Acknowledge Emotions and Move On

I would check into my intuition and feel a sensation that I should keep up my pitches to publishing houses and, in the meantime, do daily activities that seemed refreshing to my psyche. I'd schedule lunches with friends and meditate. I'd see my clients and do my presentations. I'd go on family outings. During this time, a contract job I really enjoyed as a training director, came to an end because the company I was working for closed down. It was very disheartening. I had extra time on my hands. I thought, OK, with the extra time, I will re-pitch the book. Time seemed to drag on and I'd worry. Maybe this isn't meant for me. Maybe I should do something else. For some reason, I kept at it, even though I was frustrated and discouraged. I applied the Muse Process to my own goals and, after processing and verbalizing my frustrations, I realized at some point I needed to not stay mired in the anger and frustration but use those emotions as fuel to move forward and keep at my daily activities.

Eventually, it all came together. And not in the way I had expected in my analytical way of thinking that it should turn out. I connected with my publisher via synchronicity, while I was knitting with friends. Yep, that's right; I was knitting with friends, not even thinking about the book. I was at a friend's house for a knitting group. My friend introduced me to one of her friends who was at the knitting group that day. This woman asked me what I did for a living in that casual way you do as you are chit-chatting in a group of people, not really getting in-depth but enjoying the chatter. I mentioned my book and she was curious what it was about. So I told her a bit about it, not thinking anything in particular would come of our discussion. Then she said she had met someone at Comic-Con recently representing a book publisher and asking for book manuscripts. She had lost the person's card but had remembered the name of the parent company. For those of you not familiar with Comic-Con, it is a convention dedicated to creating awareness of, and appreciation for, comics and related art forms.

I thought to myself the publisher was probably not the right one for me if it dealt with comics. I took a chance and looked it up on the

Internet anyway. It turned out that the publisher was starting a new imprint with focuses on psychology and self-help. Bingo! Life is funny that way. Sometimes it surprises you with connections you didn't consciously plan. I am here to encourage you to enjoy the process of your life as it unfolds. Think of it as an adventure. Even if you hit a discouraging point in your path, look for things to do that feed your soul and are fun and energizing. Think of how when I went knitting, not thinking it would lead to my goal, but it did. The take home point is this: it is perfectly fine to have upsetting emotions. The more you can acknowledge them, the less they will control you by knee-jerk reactions. Once you acknowledge them and process them, let them go and move forward. Do not stay stuck in the proverbial mud. I cannot tell you exactly how much time that will take for you. Everyone is unique and different in how they process emotions. Honor your own intuitive side and ask yourself, "Do I have more to process underneath or is it time to move forward now?" Really listen to what your intuition is telling you.

If you need a pick me up on your journey, here are some ideas you can do to shift your mood from discouraged to humored:

- Listen to an upbeat song.
- Jump up and down.
- Pet a dog or cat.
- Hug a friend.
- Watch a funny video.
- Laugh. Even if you are not feeling an authentic laughter, the act of laughing boosts endorphins.
- Hug a tree.
- Do something silly that you normally wouldn't (for instance, wear a kid's unicorn headband to make you laugh).
- Smile.
- Tell a friend a joke.
- Ask a friend to tell you a joke.
- Walk around the block.
- Tell yourself a joke while looking in the mirror.

PRACTICE—
ACTION PLANNER EXERCISE

Now, let's get back to action! In the Solution Generator exercise, you listed a few spontaneous action steps you can do to move toward concrete steps to your life vision. Take a moment to review what you wrote there. Tune in to your intuition and see if any additional actions steps arose. Write them all down below and commit to a completion date for each action step you write down. Write down at least three and not more than five. Creating action steps is a key component of the Muse Process. Many of my clients come for coaching solely to have accountability to take action. This activity is your accountability partner.

I commit to now completing the following action steps:

1.

2.

3.

4.

5.

I commit to completing these by this date: _____.

Think of this chapter as your very own daily accountability coach. By committing to doing a few things in the next few weeks, you will overcome inertia and begin to see your actions as seeds that start to flower.

PRACTICE—
YOUR KIND FRIEND

The next exercise is meant to access your inner resource of support. It helps to activate that motivated, helpful part of you that gets things done. You can think of it as the kindest part of you. It is that part of you that feels like a kind friend. You are going to write a letter to yourself. This is a common peak performance tool. I love teaching it to clients. It works well. I have even seen little novelty books lately with various preformatted and blank letters that you can fill out and send to yourself complete with envelopes and fancy stationery. Have a piece of blank writing paper and a pen or pencil ready—no fancy stationery required. Imagine that you are now giving yourself exactly what you wanted as you wrote down your life vision in Chapter 1. Here you can write the letter as if it is a kind friend giving you all the things you wished for or you can imagine that it is some aspect of yourself giving you all the things you wished for—in essence, a happy, healthy life. Write the letter as if it has already happened. Below is an example to get your creative juices flowing.

EXAMPLE

Dear _____ (insert your name)

I love you sooooo much! I know how much you had wanted to feel supported and loved. I know how much you had wanted to feel valued at work and to have a workplace to go to that felt supportive of you with a motivated and engaged team of colleagues. I know how much you hoped and wished for some work-life balance—to spend more fun time with your loving spouse, kids, and friends. Isn't it amazing how things have transpired for your good and now you have that amazing team of colleagues and that workplace that you are excited to get up for each day. I know you had a point in time where you felt bleak and you hated going to work each day. Now, isn't it great to literally feel like you could jump out of bed because you are so excited to get to work and work on that interesting project? And then, to top it off, to get coworkers that you love to hang out with. Can you believe you even got to plan that company holiday party that you wanted to plan? Everyone really liked it and sent you thank you notes for the time spent planning it.

Now that you are enjoying your work more, I know you sense a helpful shift in family patterns. Your spouse helps out more around the house even—wow, how did that happen? You notice you both feel a reignited heart connection—almost like a second honeymoon.

And remember that great gals-only camping trip you took with your friends? You got to reconnect with them and support each other's happiness. It was even amazing to realize you are supported even more than you thought as you felt the love of your friends. Wasn't that funny how you met up with a few extended family members that came out of the woodwork and realized they were a cool group to hang out with?

There are lots more exciting things coming up in your life as your kids grow and excel and your friends, family and coworkers celebrate all the small and large joys in life—even picnics in the park seem to take on more joy. I wish you even more joy in life, and know I am here holding space for even more joy and happiness.

Love,

Me

Now it's your turn. Get out that piece of paper and write an upbeat letter to yourself. You can use the above example as a template and tailor it to your own personal life vision come true. You can sign it as yourself or just sign the word "Me." Then, place the letter in an envelope and address it to yourself, place correct postage on it and take it to your local post office at the appointed time (do not place it in your own mailbox, be sure to take it to the postal mailbox). You get to choose when to receive it—it can be sent back in a few months or a year later. I suggest mailing it to yourself in 12 months or less. Check in with your intuition and see when it says to mail it.

You can add an additional step if you like. Read this letter to yourself in the mirror every morning for 30 days before you choose to mail it to yourself.

PRACTICE— DAILY DIARY OF GUIDED ACTIONS 30-DAY EXERCISE

Here is a calendar for you to use over the next 30 days. It has blank lines to fill in with ONE (only one) action step per day. Now you're going to access your inner success Muse when you wake up in the morning, tune in to your intuition and ask yourself, "What is the most helpful thing I can do today to achieve my goals?"

Fill in the chart for that day—every day, first thing in the morning. Remember, it can be as simple as "Go for a 10-minute walk around the block" or "Call or email my LinkedIn friend about that position today." There is a checkbox next to each day. Check off the box after you complete the action step at the end of the day. Remember to pick only one action step. This keeps it simple and keeps you motivated. Think of the old adage, "How do you eat an elephant? You eat an elephant one bite at a time."

Keep coming back to this calendar (or use the calendar in your phone) as you read through the rest of the book.

☐ DAY 1: Most important action step for today is

_____

☐ DAY 2: Most important action step for today is

_____

☐ DAY 3: Most important action step for today is

_____

☐ DAY 4: Most important action step for today is

_____

☐ DAY 5: Most important action step for today is

_____

☐ DAY 6: Most important action step for today is

_____

☐ DAY 7: Most important action step for today is

_____

☐ DAY 8: Most important action step for today is

_____

☐ DAY 9: Most important action step for today is

_____

☐ DAY 10: Most important action step for today is

_____

☐ DAY 11: Most important action step for today is

_____

☐ DAY 12: Most important action step for today is

_____

☐ DAY 13: Most important action step for today is

_____

☐ DAY 14: Most important action step for today is

_____

☐ DAY 15: Most important action step for today is

_____

☐ DAY 16: Most important action step for today is

_____

4. Getting Results by Taking Action

☐ DAY 17: Most important action step for today is

☐ DAY 18: Most important action step for today is

☐ DAY 19: Most important action step for today is

☐ DAY 20: Most important action step for today is

☐ DAY 21: Most important action step for today is

☐ DAY 22: Most important action step for today is

☐ DAY 23: Most important action step for today is

☐ DAY 24: Most important action step for today is

☐ DAY 25: Most important action step for today is

☐ DAY 26: Most important action step for today is

☐ DAY 27: Most important action step for today is

☐ DAY 28: Most important action step for today is

☐ DAY 29: Most important action step for today is

☐ DAY 30: Most important action step for today is

Isn't it great to feel like you've accomplished something? Just by reading through this book, even if you complete only a few of the action steps, you are on the way to shifting subconscious patterns to a helpful mode. Have fun with the process!

· ·

KEY TAKE-AWAYS

✓ The first key for this chapter of the book: *take one small action a day toward your life vision.*

✓ The second key for this chapter of the book: *acknowledge and express a troubling emotion.*

✓ The third key for this chapter of the book: *pick one way to move on from anger once you have expressed it.*

REFERENCES

1. Pennebaker, J.W. (1997). *Opening up: The healing power of expressing emotions, revised edition.* New York: Guilford Press.

CHAPTER 5

Focus and Unlock
Your Power

"Our deepest fear is not that we are inadequate. Our deepest fear is that we are powerful beyond measure. It is our light, not our darkness, that most frightens us."—Marianne Williamson

In this chapter, you will learn powerful focusing techniques that will unlock your power to help yourself take more purposeful actions. You will build on the meditation tools you learned in the previous chapters and personalize them even more. Over time, these tools will train your body and mind to achieve your goals and access a state of power, confidence, and visibility, even in the midst of potential stress triggers. Then, you will be less triggered by events around you and you will be able to complete your desired goals. Triggers cause subconscious reactions, which are usually counter to your desired goals. Instead of knee-jerk reactions to life events, you will learn to go into and act from an empowered, visible state. Then actions, even quick ones, will be aligned with your desired goals.

Here is the roadmap showing what you will learn in Chapter 5.

- Practice—Focus Words Exercise
- Unlocking Your Power
- Practice—Focus Points Exercise
- Practice—Positive Thoughts Lead to Positive Imagery Exercise
- Going from Invisible to Visible

PRACTICE—
FOCUS WORDS EXERCISE

When we direct our focus toward a specific goal or action, we harness the incredible power that lives within, helping us to stay committed to our vision and achieve great things. These exercises will teach you how to focus your energy and attention to activate the mighty power that exists within you.

Part One

We are going to learn Part I of the Focus Words tool to help you reach your desired goals. In Part I, you focus on a word to help you reach a relaxed alpha state. You need approximately five minutes for this exercise, but don't worry about timing it for exactly five minutes. Just flow with it and finish when you feel complete.

Read through the exercise once and then practice it with your eyes open or closed.

The Focus Word is **Calm.**

Be gentle with yourself. There is no right or wrong here. If other thoughts pop into your head during this process, let them go. Let them float off like clouds. You can keep your eyes open or closed for this exercise.

Begin to repeat your focus word, **Calm**. You can say it out loud or in your mind.

Say your focus word... Calm.

Calm... Keep gently repeating the word "Calm."

Calm ... allow a sense of calmness to wash over you...

Calm, where do you feel it in your body... Notice... Be curious...

Continue with your focus on the word Calm for a minute or two more, however long it feels right to you, and then return your full attention to the room. Open your eyes if they were closed.

For most of us with full calendars and seemingly never-ending to-do lists, our internal power is very diffused and fractured. This exercise works like a laser beam to gather your energy and direct its focus to one specific point, harnessing your power and amplifying it. The next exercise will build on this amplification.

Part Two

Now you are going to build on the Focus Words tool and personalize it even more. You will use your focus word Calm during this exercise. Over time, this exercise will train your body and mind to access a state of calm, even in the midst of potential stress triggers. For instance, you will be less triggered by events at work. Triggers cause subconscious reactions, which are usually counter to your desired goals. Instead of knee-jerk reactions to work or life events, you learn to go into and act from a calm state. Then actions, even quick ones, will be aligned with your desired goals.

NOTE: You may find it helpful to slowly read the following script a few times to get used to it, and then read it into an audio recorder to play back for yourself as you stay in a relaxed position. However, you can still learn to reach a relaxed meditative state if you choose to participate with your eyes open (or closed) without recording the script.

To begin, sit or lie down in a comfortable position and close your eyes.

Notice your body and be aware of any tension. Began releasing any tension that you notice with your breath, as you exhale (pause)... Allow your breathing to gradually slow down... As you do so, picture yourself in a garden (pause)... It is a safe place for you... The garden is very green and lovely... In the back of the garden, you may notice a gently flowing waterfall...

Imagine yourself standing in the garden.... What are you wearing? What do the plants look like ... feel like? (pause)... Can you hear the trees rustling in the breeze? Are your favorite flowers there? What do they smell like? (pause)... Feel the sun on your face... You may notice the water running down the waterfall now... The waterfall goes into a stream that contains fresh, healing spring water, taste the water if you like ... notice what it tastes like (pause)...

Allow yourself to notice if there any birds overhead. Hear the sound of the birds chirping, singing a calming song... What else do you hear in the garden? Feel the gentle breeze on your cheeks...

Imagine being barefoot in this safe garden... Notice the ground beneath your feet. How does it feel? Are you standing on the grass or on a path? Is the ground warm or cool on your feet? (pause)... Look around the garden... Choose a place in this beautiful garden to lie down...

Imagine walking to the place you have chosen and lie down there. Feel the ground beneath you. Feel the warmth of the sun and the breeze on your skin.

Enjoy the comforts of the garden ... allowing yourself to relax even more and feel safe... Notice the weight of your body resting gently and comfortably ... allowing gravity to help you release any tension and let go even more... Your body feels peaceful and calm ... allowing you to relax and release even more...

Feel the sun above your head warming you and further relaxing you. Breathe in the warmth and vibrancy of the sun, allow it to fill you with a sense of calm and peace from the top of your head to the tips of your toes. Notice as you become part of your safe garden that you feel more rested, more relaxed, more at peace...

Now, in this safe, calm place ... place a movie screen in front of you and imagine a time in the past when you felt unsettled or uncomfortable with work or business ... place this scene on your movie screen … watch the movie as a distant observer of this scene… Notice what other people were doing or saying, notice what you were doing or saying…

Now imagine that the "calm" you, the one watching the movie, steps in and replaces the "old" you in the movie. Allow yourself to focus on your breathing and imagine the word "calm." Hear it … feel its resonance … feel your breathing, notice it slows, see yourself as calm, what does that look like? (pause)… What does that feel like?… Say "I am calmer" … "I am more relaxed" … "I naturally gravitate to pleasant, prosperous work." Replay the scene again, this time with the "calm" you… Notice the difference… How do you sound different?… Feel different… How do others look?… Feel different?… Notice the temperature… The feel of the air on your skin… Even notice the smell of the air around you … as you feel calmer… Feel your focus word Calm (pause) … feeling more and more relaxed (pause)… Allow yourself to stay with this calm feeling for a few moments here, as you leave the scene and rest quietly… (Pause for about a minute)

When you feel ready, leave this meditation scene and sit for a few moments more. Then take a few minutes to reflect on your experience during the exercise.

Action Step
1. How do you feel after the Focus Words exercise? More relaxed? Note any changes, even slight ones, here.

2. Practice the Focus Words exercise twice this week (or more if you'd like). Notice and be curious of positive work or life shifts. Note a few shifts, even slight ones, here.

UNLOCKING YOUR POWER

The next tool is called Focus Points. It is another option to reach a natural, focused state of mind to achieve your desired goals in your life vision. There are several points on the body that are useful to focus on that help you reach a meditative state and focus you more clearly on your emerging life vision. These points are derived from acupressure practices. It is a very powerful tool for lessening life stress and reaching a state of peak performance as well.

Before we get started, I want to give you some background, share with you some research and theory on acupressure, and tell you how it works to help you be your best. Several thousand years ago practitioners of what is now called acupuncture discovered points on the body that could be used for physical and emotional healing and balance. From these ancient practitioners, the current techniques of acupuncture and acupressure were born. The most commonly held definitions define acupressure points as specific points or places on the skin that are especially sensitive to bioelectrical impulses in the body.[1] These places on the skin are the junctures or intersections of special pathways, called meridians, which carry the vital life force or "Qi." Qi, also spelled as "Chi," is our vital life force energy, according to acupressure philosophy. When these acupressure points are stimulated, it assists your body in self-regulating and also with balancing your emotional state and focus.

I have developed a metaphor for this system to make it simple to understand and apply in your daily life. Let's imagine that the meridians are busy roads. The junctures, or acupressure points, are the traffic lights where the roads intersect. The traffic on the road is the bioelectrical life force or Qi. Stimulating the points is analogous to traffic lights changing from red to green, allowing the "traffic" (vital life force) to continue to flow. When there is a blockage or imbalance at a point, it's like a traffic jam or a red light.

Studies show that acupuncture works with the electrical system within our bodies. It's a simple process that is complicated to explain, so I'm not going to go into it here, but if you want to learn about it in more detail, I've included some great resources in the Additional Resources at the end of the book. Essentially, what I can tell you is that when you focus on a point on the body by doing acupressure, it is the same process as meditation. You are *focusing on one thing* for a period of time in order to induce a focused state of awareness. These points work on many different levels to help you have a happy and balanced life.

PRACTICE— FOCUS POINTS EXERCISE

Part One

There are several acupressure points on the body that can help calm your mind and shift your mindset naturally. You are now going to learn about two points you can quickly use to reach a calm and focused state of mind. You can hold these points with your eyes open or closed.

Point I

The first point is called the Third Eye Point. This point is located between the eyebrows, basically in the indentation where the bridge of the nose starts. Place any finger at the point between your eyebrows and apply gentle pressure for approximately two minutes. Focus your attention on this point as you hold it.

Point II

The second point is called the Sea of Tranquility Point. This point is located on the center of the breastbone. You can place three fingers vertically at the center of the breastbone to ensure you are contacting the correct point. Hold this point with gentle pressure for about two minutes. Focus your attention on this point as you hold it.

The point of this exercise is to focus your attention on the general area of the points. If you are unsure of the exact location of the point, just bringing your focus to the general area there will work fine. However, if you would like to see a diagram of the two points, please visit my website at www.drbarbaracox.com.

Part Two

Start by touching the spot right between your eyebrows, in the indentation where the bridge of the nose begins. It is best to use the middle finger at the spot and hold it with gentle pressure. Hold for at least two minutes. As you focus on this point, allow your imagination go to your safe garden. Let feelings of relaxation wash over you. Then bring your life vision and goals into awareness. Imagine you have achieved all that you wanted. You can be happy with all the wonderful things in your life. You can close your eyes for a moment as you do this exercise. What does that feel like?

When you feel complete, release the point and note any insights and feelings you had below.

Action Step

1. How do you feel after the Focus Points exercise? Are you more relaxed? Note any changes, even slight ones, here:

2. Practice the Focus Points exercise twice this week (or more if you'd like). Notice and be curious of positive shifts in your life. Note a few things you notice throughout the week below.

PRACTICE—
POSITIVE THOUGHTS LEAD
TO POSITIVE IMAGERY EXERCISE

Psychological research shows that when we are children, before we develop verbal language, we process our experiences into pictures and body sensations and then store them in our memory. Therefore, imagery is the primary source of information for us prior to the development of language. Focusing on images or body sensations enables us to reach a primary, non-verbal level of subconscious memory. Thus, using imagery in this way helps you to anchor a desired pattern change into your unconscious as well as your conscious mind. This tool, called Positive Thoughts Lead to Positive Imagery, will teach you how to make positive thoughts work for you.

For this exercise, you will pick one short, negative thought and associated sensory image you have had about work or about how work affects other aspects of your life. Then you will pick one short, reframed positive thought and associated image you have about work. First, follow along with the example below in order to help you pick a personalized thought and personalized sensory image for this exercise.

EXAMPLE
(See chart on top of following page.)

EXAMPLE
For this exercise, pick one short, negative thought you have had about work or about how work affects other aspects of your life. Note it in the space below, along with the first negative image that pops into your mind. If you would like to keep it simple, you can use Jenny's negative phrase and image and tailor it to your situation—"I will *always* be stressed at work or in life" and "I see/hear my supervisor's voice criticizing me."

Next, pick one short, reframed positive thought you have about

Practice—Positive Thoughts Lead to Positive Imagery Exercise

Jenny's Positive Thought/Positive Imagery Flow Chart

Negative Thought:	Associated Negative Imagery:	Positive Thought:	Associated Positive Imagery:
I will *always* feel stressed at this workplace.	I see my boss (I hear her critical voice) who is living rent-free in my head.	I don't have to take one person's opinion as a measure of my work success. I remember that, even though we all make mistakes, I actually do several things well. There are times I feel calm at work.	I hear myself saying goodbye to my boss's voice in my head and I see myself showing her out the door. I sense myself feeling calmer. I am smiling.

work. State it in such a way that you could believe it at least sometimes. Note it in the space below, along with the first positive image that pops into your mind. Again, feel free to use Jenny's example as a template— "I sometimes enjoy work" and "I sense and see myself feeling calmer."

Negative Thought:

Associated Negative Imagery:

Positive Thought:

Associated Positive Imagery:

5. Focus and Unlock Your Power

Action Step

1. How do you feel after doing this exercise? Note any beneficial changes, even slight ones, below.

2. Practice the Positive Thought/Positive Imagery focus tool twice this week (or more if you'd like). Notice and be curious of positive shifts in your life. Note a few below as your week progresses.

3. Notice one or two times you feel relatively calm or happy at work this week, and write down

- what you are doing;

- one sentence on what you are saying to yourself (your self-talk); and

- what you are picturing and sensing (use all five senses).

GOING FROM INVISIBLE TO VISIBLE

We have discussed how you can learn new tools that help you move from feeling disempowered to feeling empowered in your daily life. By making this shift, you can have enjoyable relationships and fulfilling families and careers that are suited to your unique personality.

One way to learn empowerment is to acknowledge beliefs and patterns in your life that were developed in the past but continue to keep you from living up to your life potential. Then challenge these false thoughts and patterns, like we did in the above exercise when we learned how Jenny challenged and shifted these thoughts. This process can evoke unpleasant feelings such as anger or frustration, maybe even a sense of unfairness, as we noted. The journey of moving from feeling invisible to feeling visible in society includes acknowledging those frustrating feelings. You learned tools to verbalize and to release those feelings. This process may take you a day, a month, or longer—it's like brushing your teeth regularly. Check in with your feelings on a regular basis and ask yourself what you need to express.

It is a process of finding your voice to become more visible, to speak your truth when you need to say, "This or that situation in my life is not right—let's change it." It boils down to defining your space and your values. It is recognizing what you will and will not tolerate and being OK with it. Heck, it took me more than five years to write this book, so I was processing these frustrated feelings as I went through the book writing journey. Just be gentle with yourself. In doing this work, I have come to truly understand that you don't have to sweep anger under the rug—it can motivate you to do great things. However, acknowledging unpleasant feelings and releasing them to achieve a pleasant state of visibility does not have to take years.

I see a common theme when women begin to ask for what they want in life and start stepping out to become more visible. Some women have a learned belief, probably stemming from childhood, that "girls shouldn't ask for what they want" and "I should blend in." This fear of visibility and of speaking your truth can impact women in terms of pay raises, job promotions, or better treatment in relationships in general. This fear seems to arise from that part of us that represents our inner child. At our core, everyone wants to be liked and accepted, men and women. It is a legacy of our evolution, as we evolved to be included in an interdependent tribe. However, if left unchecked, this tendency can lead to us blending in too much and losing our visibility in the world. We as women really need to bring this unconscious knee-jerk reaction forward to our conscious mind. It includes being gentle with yourself and noticing when your inner child rears her head, so to speak. Whenever you feel that little twinge of "I need to get that person's approval"—just take a step back and notice it. The act of stepping back and noticing the need for approval starts to defuse it, so that it will not control you.

5. Focus and Unlock Your Power

As the famous psychologist Viktor Frankl said, "Between stimulus and response there is a space. In that space is our power to choose our response. In our response lies our growth and our freedom." That way you can act from a conscious place, not react from an unconscious place. Again, we all crave some level of approval; it is a basic human need to be interconnected with others. You are not meant to live on an island alone. You would get tired and lonely. However, refuse to let your every movement be dictated by your inner child. Start to become more consciously aware of when your inner approval beacon goes off. Your inner child may want your boss to approve of you. The boss may not have given you a raise or promotion in a while. It may feel like he doesn't notice you. This need for approval may hinder you from asking for visibility in the form of a raise or promotion. One thing I have learned in 20 years of doing this work is that people hang out in their own internal universe, whether they are bosses, CEOs, or somebody others we may think is "more important." Basically, people are 99 percent of the time thinking about their own needs and worries, their own deadlines and whatever else they need to get done. Your boss is probably thinking, "What do I need to get from the grocery store tonight?" or "Am I going to get home in time to get my kid to soccer practice?" or whatever else happens in their daily activities.

Start to notice that even the people you think are higher up or more important than you are regular people too. Remember, they have to get dressed and brush their teeth just like you do in the morning. If you are running around stressed and worried about your own problems and thinking that no one gives you the credit you deserve, they are most likely thinking the same exact type of thoughts. It's just human nature. In fact, I would bet a million dollars that they are doing the same thing as you.

When you do start to realize this fact more often in your own life, then you won't start to place people above you, or think of them as superior to you or you inferior to them. You will begin to notice that we are all on equal footing. As human beings, we all eat and breathe and have a basic human need to connect and be loved.

This is the place of awareness that is helpful to be anchored to in your conscious mind. It will help you move into a place of acting from more self-esteem and visibility. More and more often, you will realize you are just as valuable as the next person, whether it is your boss, your neighbor, your spouse or your kids. This is a very important mindset to adopt.

As you may have discovered as you read this book, I like to keep things lighthearted, even serious topics like self-confidence, so the next time you feel a twinge of insecurity in asking for visibility like a raise or for that corner office, simply envision the other person putting their pants on one leg at a time—while running around trying to brush his teeth in the morning and attempting not to be late to work. By doing this little mental rehearsal, you can approach your life vision and goals with more humor. Even something as serious sounding as a life vision can be guided by lightheartedness. Tune in to that part of you that is lighthearted and confident.

As I always tell my clients, there's at least one time in your life that you felt a glimmer of self-confidence. I imagine there is probably more than one time that you felt that spark of self-confident visibility. Think back to that … what did it feel like?

Let me share a story from my own personal experience when I doubted my own self-confidence. I had to remind myself of my inner glimmer of self-confidence many times as I started my first job right out of college. I was a twenty-something, a shy, petite blonde gal working in a primarily male-dominated field. I did environmental work for the Department of Defense. My role entailed inspections of all of the public works department's metal finishing shops and other repair shops.

When I started, I had bouts of insecurity since I was one of the only females doing that particular job. These bouts manifested as self-doubt, negative self-talk, and taking a passive approach to my job (like not speaking up when I needed to). I knew that I needed to change, so I tried something new. To help bolster my self-esteem and raise my comfort around being visible, I started to help myself by just connecting with other women who I felt were a bit more confident than me so that I could emulate what they were doing. There was one other woman that started a few months before me and was my age. So I glommed onto her, at times like she was my only hope. I considered her a role model or a template that I could model myself after. We also supported one another. She was my first glimmer of any type of professional female community. Later, I also joined activities like Toastmasters to help me improve my self-confidence. This was my first career-related opportunity learning to tune in to my inner self-confident state.

Just like other states we have been discussing, self-confidence is a state of mind. And it can be learned and taught. Anytime you need a quick boost of confidence, think back to a time where you felt super confident. Imagine you're doing a self-confidence meditation. Just by tuning into how you feel in your body, when you think back to that self-confident time you can train your body to have a pattern of self-confidence. It can be as easy as that. Like everything it wouldn't hurt to do a little practice. Before you go to bed at night, think of about what it feels like to be super confident the next day. I know you can do it.

I believe in the mind-body connection and in the power of your mindset to make change in your life, such as boosting your sense of visibility. I know it works, but some people need more evidence. If you want more proof, here is a great example that demonstrates how what you consciously choose to think alters and impacts your physical world. This simple mental activity below illustrates the connection between your mind, your thoughts, and your physical reactions to your thoughts.

Imagine you are holding a freshly-picked, juicy, bright yellow lemon in your hand. Allow yourself to feel its texture and see the brightness of its yellow skin. Imagine you are going to use the lemon for some tasty dinner preparation. Put the lemon on a cutting board and begin to slice it into four parts.

As you do so, feel the juice squirting out of it. Pick up a lemon wedge and smell it—do you notice the citrus fragrance? Taste the lemon and let the juices run over your tongue. Suck on the lemon and taste the sour, tart flavor... Notice what happens in your mouth and body... Your cheeks may pucker and you may salivate heavily in response to the sour taste. Scan your mouth and body and notice your reactions and sensations.

What actual physical changes did you notice in your body while you were imagining this? For example, extra saliva, a twinge in your cheeks, or anything else?

By using your mind and an imaginary lemon, you were able to produce real biochemical, physical changes in your body. In this same way, you can harness the power of your mind to create healthy subconscious patterns and habits. People are always surprised about how much their thoughts *do* in fact affect their bodies and their physical behaviors. This mental activity is proof that your imagination does produce changes in your physical world. You can harness the power of your mind and your imagination to produce both mental and physical changes in your life to raise your visibility. And you can use this power to enhance and increase your personal happiness and effectiveness in your world.

Start simple with the process of being visible in the world. How about saying, "I love you—it is OK to be seen" to yourself in the mirror when you wake up every morning? Even though it may feel unfamiliar, you can produce physical changes by saying and thinking these thoughts on a regular basis. They can become a natural habit and state.

I really do believe that, no matter what unpleasantness people have experienced in the past, they can recover from that and move on. They can learn to hold pleasant states of mind on a regular basis. Our brains and bodies are remarkably regenerative. You can and will regenerate from whatever disappointments or visibility fears you experienced in the past. You can move into new awareness of peaceful relating and happy experiences in your career and life.

Proof That Women Are Becoming More Visible and Valued

Let's start this shift into more visibility and flow at work and in life by looking at some research and data showing that shifts have indeed already occurred. We will start with education. It is exciting to note that female education levels have improved considerably of the past several years. For instance in South Asia, Africa, and the Middle East, girls' primary school enrollment rates doubled in the second half of the 20th century, rising faster than boys' enrollment rates and substantially reducing gender gaps in schooling.[2] In addition, more than half a billion women have joined the world's labor force over the past 30 years.[3] In terms of women's rights, almost every country in the world has now ratified the Convention on the Elimination of All Forms of Discrimination Against Women.[4] A recent research study showed that greater gender equality enhances a country's economic efficiency and quality of life. Researchers found that as more women are employed across the world, economies have flourished.[5] These studies highlight the fact that women are becoming more visible and valued in the world.

Women are also more successful in the workplace than they have ever been before. Interesting data from a *Harvard Business Review* article[6] entitled "Women in the Workplace: A Research Roundup" on leadership effectiveness evaluations revealed, "At every management level, the women were rated higher than the men." Not only were the women judged to be superior in areas where women are traditionally thought to excel, such as developing others and building relationships, but their ratings were significantly higher, statistically speaking, on several traits identified, in more than 30 years of research, as "most important to overall leadership effectiveness."

Another study found that as more women enter the workforce, wages rise, including for men![7]

This data illustrates that women are truly gaining visibility for the skills and talents they bring to the table. True and lasting positive change comes from noticing any and all positive shifts in your life—even small shifts. Get together with other women who are celebrating the positive visibility shifts in their communities and their lives. The data clearly shows that we are becoming more visible in the workplace and can now own our power. We are moving into a time where things that used to be covered up and hidden are now brought into the light and addressed. I invite you to release that old resentment around feeling invisible or unvalued. Make space for the new improvements that are already here in the world and the wonderful things that are happening in your world.

PRACTICE—
BECOMING VISIBLE

In this section, you learn some tools to practice feeling comfortable becoming more visible. We prepare by doing a quick Body Tune-In exercise.

Preparation

Remember this body tune-in helps you to shift unconscious patterns. Let's set the intention that this tune-in will help clear any unconscious fears about becoming too visible. Since you have practiced it in Chapter 2, you are probably able to do this exercise in just a few minutes:

Take a deep breath ... inhale ... and pause for a beat at the top ... now exhale through the mouth, pausing for a beat at the bottom... Do that one more time slowly ... inhale ... and pause for a beat at the top... Now exhale through the mouth, pausing for a beat at the bottom. And one more big deep breath ... inhale ... and pause for a beat at the top... Now exhale through the mouth, pausing for a beat at the bottom. And as you continue, make the exhale a little longer than the inhale...

Continue with these deep breaths, and tune in to your tailbone. Feel the chair holding you, making contact with your muscles. Gently move your tailbone back and forth, feeling that space ground you and center you...

Continue your deep breaths, and move your focus up to your body center, right inside your belly ... feel the muscles in your core contract for a moment ... focus on the strength that it gives your entire body...

5. Focus and Unlock Your Power

As you continue your deep breaths, work your way up toward your rib cage, focus on your solar plexus, which is the spot right between your ribs ... feel it engage while you inhale and exhale ... feel how it helps your breath flow through your body...

And continue to take more deep breaths while you shift your focus to your heart ... concentrate on the lightness you feel deep in your chest ... notice how it rises and falls with every inhale and exhale...

And as you take another deep breath, move your focus to your throat ... sense how the energy in your throat expands as you connect to it ... sense how any blocks you might feel in your communication start to dissipate ... feel the channels of communication start to open and notice your internal voice strengthening...

Continue your deep breaths and now shift your focus up to the spot on your forehead right between your eyes ... feel a lightness fill your body when you focus here ... feel how it clears your mind, relaxes your jaw, and softens your shoulders...

Now take another deep breath and tune in to the point just above your head... Feel a positive current run through your body, a gold-like energy running up and down ... sense how your body lifts and expands, and notice how you stand taller and stretch your spine to touch that point...

Take one more deep breath and imagine yourself connected to all seven points at the same time ... inhale ... and pause for a beat at the top... Now exhale through the mouth, pausing for a beat at the bottom. You are now tuned in to your body. You may even feel lighter and more energized.

Becoming Visible with a Focus Word

Now that you are in tune with your body, we are going to add a new focus word to your repertoire. The focus word is **Visible**.

Remember to flow with this exercise and finish when you feel complete. Read through the exercise once and then practice it with your eyes open or closed.

Be gentle with yourself. There is no right or wrong here. If other thoughts pop into your head during this process, let them go. Let them float off like clouds. You can keep your eyes open or closed for this exercise.

Begin to repeat your focus word, "**Visible**." You can say it out loud or in your mind.

Say your focus word… Visible.

Visible… Keep gently repeating the word "Visible."

Visible … allow a sense of peace to wash over you as you become more Visible…

Visible, where do you feel it in your body… Notice… Be curious…

Continue with your focus on the word "Visible" for a minute or two more, however long it feels right to you, and then return your full attention to the room. Open your eyes if they were closed.

Creating Your Own Focus Word

In this section, you can choose your own personalized focus word and practice it here. I invite you to choose a word that helps you feel more visible or empowered.

My focus word is _____. (Fill in all blank lines with your personal focus word.)

Remember to flow with this exercise and finish when you feel complete.

Read through the exercise once and then practice it with your eyes open or closed.

Be gentle with yourself. There is no right or wrong here. If other thoughts pop into your head during this process, let them go. Let them float off like clouds. You can keep your eyes open or closed for this exercise.

Begin to repeat your focus word, _____. You can say it out loud or in your mind.

Say your focus word … _____.

_____… Keep gently repeating the word "_____."

_____ … allow a sense of peace to wash over you as you become more _____…

_____, where do you feel it in your body… Notice… Be curious…

Continue with your focus on the word "_____" for a minute or two more, however long it feels right to you, and then return your full attention to the room. Open your eyes if they were closed.

You did it! You have now aligned your body and mind to achieve your action steps and goals more readily and to be in a state of power, confidence, and visibility. All of the processes and exercises are working together to regularly activate your own inner success Muse. In the next chapter, you can start to gather collaborative and reciprocal people around you and help propel each other to your life vision.

· ·

KEY TAKE-AWAYS

✓ The first key for this chapter of the book: *you learned several techniques to use the focused power of alpha state meditation to own your power and take action. Pick your favorite one and practice it a few times this week.*

✓ The second key for this chapter of the book: *according to statistics, women are becoming more visible and valued in the world.*

References

1. Gach, M.R. (1990). *Acupressure's potent points: A guide to self-care for common ailments*. New York: Bantam Books.

2. Improving women's lives: Progress and obstacles. http://siteresources.world bank.org/INTGENDER/Resources/Chapter2.pdf. Worldbank.Org. Retrieved 05/03/18.

3. Revenga, A., & Shetty, S. (2012). Empowering women is smart economics. *International Monetary Fund*, 49(1). Retrieved from http://www.imf.org/external/pubs/ft/fandd/2012/03/revenga.htm.

4. Revenga, A., & Shetty, S. (2012). Empowering women is smart economics. *International Monetary Fund*, 49(1). Retrieved from http://www.imf.org/external/pubs/ft/fandd/2012/03/revenga.htm.

5. Facts and Figures: Economic Empowerment. (2017, July). In *UNWomen*. Retrieved from http://www.unwomen.org/en/what-we-do/economic-empowerment/facts-and-figures.

6. Women in the workplace: A research roundup. (2013, September). *Harvard Business Review*. Retrieved from https://hbr.org/2013/09/women-in-the-workplace-a-research-roundup.

7. Weinstein, A. (2018, January 31). When more women join the workforce, wages rise—including for men. *Harvard Business Review*. Retrieved from https://hbr.org/2018/01/when-more-women-join-the-workforce-wages-rise-including-for-men?autocomplete=true.

CHAPTER 6

Cultivating Collaboration and Tribe

"Surround yourself with only people who are going to lift you higher."—Oprah Winfrey

Community building and collaboration are key aspects of the integrated feminine archetype of your success Muse app. In this chapter, we will discuss how to build a collaborative group in your life—those people who want you to be relaxed and happy, those people who are excited for you to have exactly what you want in work and life. We're going to touch on some key concepts about how you can start building a reciprocal community that helps everyone involved accomplish goals. To illustrate this, there is an in-depth case study. This real-life example will model collaborative behaviors for you and help you learn to integrate these mindsets into your own life.

Here is the roadmap showing what you will learn in Chapter 6.

- Cultivating Collaboration in Your Life

- Case Study—Sabrina's Confidence and New Connections

- Practice—Connecting to Your Tribe Meditation Exercise

CULTIVATING COLLABORATION IN YOUR LIFE

This chapter will raise awareness of how we can bring in more community and collaboration to enjoy your daily work and life.

What is a collaborative community—those people that want you to be relaxed and happy and have exactly what you want! Community is what makes things work well. Connecting to like-minded groups helps things flow for everyone involved. We are not meant to be an isolated bunch of individuals bumping into each other and feeling annoyed when we bump into each other, and then continuing our own individual lonely existence. We evolved to be individuals in an interconnected web of existence, where we each celebrate our beautiful individuality as a unique expression of life. We can then celebrate how all our wonderful puzzle pieces of individuality connect in an interdependent network.

There is a public health crisis called loneliness in our society. Loneliness stems from lack of community. Much research from the past several years has shown that over the past three decades, American social organizations have declined in membership. It was slowly starting to pick up in the past decade. The research highly recommended we reconnect for health and vitality of our communities and our lives.

Loneliness leads to stress, health problems, and a feeling of existential angst. One of the key pillars of the Muse Process is to connect—to remember that you are part of this interconnected web of existence called community. You can solve this public health crisis solely by remembering this fact. What if each of us suddenly remembered that we have evolved to be connected in a tribe? I know a cascade effect will happen where people realize at a gut level that community means flow. That is the most important piece of information in this entire chapter, so let me repeat it again ... community means flow.

When you're part of a community, you have support. You have cheerleaders. You have people who will lend an ear, give a word of encouragement, and act as a sounding board or brainstorming partner to help you work through your thoughts and ideas. You will see that it is much easier to accomplish tasks and get things done with enjoyable company along the way. There is no law against having fun or getting help—in fact, this is necessary to be successful in life! I learned this as I was older. I was a serious child, so I am having my childhood in reverse and learning to have fun along with you!

Examples of Collaboration in Action

One of the best examples of this in action is when neighbors or even entire neighborhoods decide to collaborate on dinner prep. I've visited places where neighbors coordinate meals together and sometimes they even build neighborhoods where they share a common house or clubhouse in a planned community. The babysitting room or exercise room in the clubhouse is converted to a large kitchen where the whole neighborhood plans one to five meals a week cafeteria-style. I was curious about the public health research that shows people are healthier when they have connections—when they are part of community organizations, such as civic organizations, volunteer organizations, or spiritual organizations—so I took a road trip to research community and see the different forms it took. The people who had more collaborative support, and made community connection a vital part of their lives, had the most enjoyable and productive lives.

Let's take a closer look at the example I noted above, where one neighborhood had five meals a week together in their community clubhouse. Each family in the neighborhood agreed to cook one meal a month at the clubhouse. There are approximately 40 houses in this example. Another family agreed to clean up after the family that cooked the meal. They had an online calendar to sign up to host cooking or cleaning. If you volunteer to be in the rotation, then you go to the clubhouse to eat dinner most every night—to have a home-cooked meal prepared and ready when you got home from work—and you only have to cook dinner approximately once a month. Everyone who lived in this neighborhood said it was the most amazing time-saving arrangement.

They also had a sign-up sheet in the clubhouse to rotate babysitting for families that had children. Anybody that wanted to be a part of it could drop off their kids at a certain time of the day and have complimentary babysitting if they also signed up for a rotation. If you like this scenario, you could adopt a version of it for yourself and your neighbors, modifying it for your own community's needs.

For me, the issue of community was most important after the birth of my daughter. We wanted to forge more connections and attend more social events in order to feel this sense of supportive tribe, especially with raising children. As the old adage goes, it takes a village to raise a child. Our plan in building a collaborative community was to move from the suburbs into a more community-oriented urban area. I most definitely think you can set up more community in the suburbs and I hope that people will. But for us at that time, we were also very passionate about being kinder to the environment and we wanted to limit our use to one car. Therefore, we wanted to be somewhere we could walk to restaurants and the grocery store. We also bought a multi-unit property because we thought it would be fun to have like-minded people who wanted to build community living nearby. As happens with some of my projects, it turned into a major undertaking. But that was just because we bought a fixer-upper for the triplex. I spent the next several years coordinating contractors to fix it up. Eventually, we got it fixed up and we found some like-minded renters and collected various friends who were into community events and potlucks. At the time that I conceived of this venture, we decided to have one potluck a month. So we invited our friends and neighbors to come over for a potluck and a game night to build more connections and cross connections for other people. I've found that people who live in cities can go years without getting to know their neighbors. I encourage you to counter this trend, and just say hello to somebody that you see every day that you might have passed for years and not said anything to before.

In our scenario for the social community-building experiment that I did, we held monthly potlucks and asked everyone who attended to bring something to share. By building this community, I was able to meet new colleagues, save time in meal preparation, and just get to know my neighbors better, which significantly increased my quality of life in the neighborhood.

That example is here to get your creative juices flowing. You may set it up a different way than I did. You may already have something like that going on in your own neighborhood—or something even better going on.

My purpose in writing this chapter is to be a beacon of hope for more community collaboration and connection. As I noted earlier, the feminine archetypal qualities we could stand to bring in more of are the qualities of intuition, community, and collaboration. These qualities propel us to our best life vision.

Another idea for more community and collaboration is the new social trend of co-working. I know many of my millennial clients do this, where they work in shared work spaces. This shared space provides a way for people to find camaraderie, ask for help, brainstorm with experts in other industries, network, and get support overall. With so many people working outside the office now, a shared co-working arrangement gives people a place to connect and helps fight loneliness that can come when you work at home.

More Ways to Acknowledge Your Connections

Sometimes I've noticed a trend especially for women that we feel like we have to do it all alone—or that something is wrong with us if we want help. However, remember that it is a perfectly natural biological predisposition to do things in a tribe and get help. In addition, research shows that children who are raised in a connected community with lots of loving adult figures in their lives to help out do better.

Nowadays with our modern society set up as it is, we need to put just a little extra attention and love into building our own tribe. We need to be intentional about it. With many families spread out across the distances, community support is not often as built in as it used to be 50 or 100 years ago. At present, we have to put thought into how to connect with our tribe consistently.

Just to start thinking about it, spend a few moment journaling about your tribe.

- What types of people are in your chosen tribe?
- How do you feel in that chosen tribe?
- What do you do together?
- Anything else?

After you journal about your tribe in general, I recommend identifying some people you already know who would be in your tribe. Especially if you have children or are planning to have children in the future, one vital activity I always recommend my clients do is to identify five people you can count on for community. Who are five people you can ask for support? You can collaborate and support them too. Some examples are to swap babysitting, pick each other up from the airport, and help out in times of sickness. List those five people here:

1.

2.

3.

4.

5.

If you can't think of five people that's OK. We will hone your intuition later on in this chapter.

This is where the concepts of intuition, community, and collaboration connect. I encourage you to honor your intuition and let it lead you to your community. Your community may end up looking different than you originally thought it would.

I know it did for me. When I originally decided to have children, I didn't realize how important community would be in a work-life balance. When I was in my 30s, due to various circumstances, many of my friends did not have children. I had a rosy image in my mind that I would have several close friends with children and we would all raise our children together. As fate would have it, unfortunately, that is not how my early child-rearing years went. However, over several years I ended up meeting a few very nice women through my daughter's school and we would occasionally swap sleepover babysitting nights.

Community also helps you to build more self-care into your own life. Self-care is vital in moving forward in your life vision and career. Also, realize that in taking good care of yourself, you are a better functioning member of your tribe. In your life vision activity, especially if you have children or are planning to soon, as part of your work-life balance initiative, I'd like you to ponder how you can build in self-care and reflect on the question "How will I build self-care for myself as I raise my children and continue my career?"

Everyone's answer to this is different. For my coaching clients, many schedule a night out with friends once a week or once a month. That is one common way to building self-nurturance. Self-nurturance is vital in your life vision. Taking care of yourself is just like the oxygen mask at 32,000 feet that I mentioned earlier. You need your oxygen to feel good and stay motivated. Plus, it's a good example for your children and for others. Here is where you can speak to your subconscious about the importance of self-care, and let it know this so you can ditch any guilt you might feel when you take time for yourself. Go ahead … you have my permission to let it go.

Here is something I invite you to try this week. Every morning, mindfully put on lipstick or lip balm for a minute. How does it feel to take care of yourself in this way? How does it feel to take a moment to do something for yourself? Use putting on lipstick as a meditative activity. Really feel putting on the lipstick … notice how it glides on … notice the texture, notice the color, notice the smell, even. While you are doing this, think to yourself, "I love you. I thank you. I'm going to take good care of you." If this feels uncomfortable at first you can add "so that you can take good care of others too." This activity honors caring for yourself, which also honors caring for your community.

Birds of a Feather Flock Together

Everyone in a group of people reinforces everyone else's belief system. By spending time with one another, we start to think alike and hold the same values and beliefs. When people you spend time with keep talking about their struggles and drama that grows in focus. I'm not saying there are never difficult things in life, but what you focus on grows.

Spend a bit more time talking about something uplifting in your groups. Spend a bit more time talking about something pleasant in your life—it can be anything like "Wasn't it lovely how the birds were chirping this morning?" or "Wasn't the sunny weather just beautiful today?" or "I am so happy my _____ (fill in the blank) is good!" This causes you to move into the positive more and attract more of those people into your sphere. Those people tend to reinforce your improved state of mind. Usually, they don't enjoy complaining for an hour about how crummy life is; they'd rather spend that hour, for example, taking a walk at the beach, which boosts endorphins and mood.

If talking about something pleasant (or even finding something pleasant) to talk about is hard for you, it means you have to do it more often—practice, find someone, just one person, that does this better than you or more often and spend more time with that person. Meet for coffee or tea, talk on the phone, go for a walk or go to the gym, whatever—just hang out with that person. This is the easiest and best thing you can do for yourself. Model how this person talks. Write down a few things you notice that she talks about.

-

-

-

-

Add another positive-speaking person to your circle of acquaintances next week. Notice what she talks about.

-

-

-

-

By now, you should notice changes to your life in a happier direction.

CASE STUDY—
SABRINA'S CONFIDENCE
AND NEW CONNECTIONS

We're going to touch on a few concepts about how you can start building a reciprocal group of connections that helps you all accomplish your goals and live your life visions. To illustrate this, we use a case study.

Sabrina was a 52-year-old sales executive who presented as a very elegant and experienced woman. However, she felt she had a need to improve her self-esteem and confidence in presenting to higher-ups. She'd been in sales about 15 years and had done well enough to receive promotions, but she wanted to improve. Sabrina felt that her lack of confidence in presenting to clients had cost her sales. In an effort to help her improve, Sabrina's company contracted with me. It wanted her work with me to build her confidence around sales confidence and presentations to clients.

During our work together, Sabrina and I went through the five-step process outlined in this book—I taught her how to connect to her success muse, go into an alpha state, and picture what she wanted to accomplish. By the fifth session, Sabrina was feeling so much more confident that her sales increased significantly; she realized that by the first quarter, she even exceeded her quota by 102 percent, which had never happened before.

Part of Sabrina's work during our coaching was connected to her desire to build her social and professional network, a reciprocal tribe for her work and family life, which the alpha state confidence pattern helped. Sabrina noted after learning the tools, for example, she went to a trade show and connected with several doctors to present her products.

After she did the exercises to reach a meditative state, her creative unconscious prompted her to connect with more social groups. When she came out of the alpha state, she reported this finding to me and I asked her to identify two groups she wanted to connect with that week. She chose two possibilities and attended those meetings. From doing the Muse Process, she connected with more potential clients and found another healthcare provider that had a need for her products.

By learning the alpha state process, which put her in a more confident state of mind, and using this confidence pattern to lead her to the most appropriate social groups to connect with, Sabrina was able to identify more targeted leads that resulted in a notable increase in her sales. If she would have connected with social groups before going through the alpha state process and shifting her mindset to confidence, it might not have worked as well. Sabrina had previously had a difficult time connecting with people. Her shift in mindset opened the door for her to connect on a more personal level with new networks, which was a key reason she was able to turn these leads into sales and build her professional network. In this process, it is important to do the alpha state activity before building your community. This allows you to achieve different results with these new reciprocal connections than you would have without the process.

For Sabrina, when she paired the two steps together—alpha state and building her community—it amplified her personal change and led to greater results. She met and connected with people that were a win-win for everyone.

The case study shows that integrating this process led her to connect to social groups and individuals that were aligned with her goals, values, and life vision. Her shift in mindset opened the door for her to connect on a more personal level with new supportive networks, which was a key reason she achieved her goals and had more life satisfaction. In this process, it's important to do the alpha state process and shift your mindset before building new components to your community. This allows you to achieve different results from these new connections than you would have without the process—results that reciprocally benefit both you and the connections.

Try it yourself!

To get you ready for the next activity, let's do our Relaxed Breathing exercise.

Our breathing pattern can be more noticeable when we are lying down and in a quiet location.

So if you are able, lie comfortably on the floor, place one hand on your upper chest and the other hand on your belly.

For now, breathe how you normally would and notice which hand rises and falls the most.

If you are currently tense or anxious, you tend to breathe from the chest with short, shallow breaths.

If you notice that you are breathing from the chest, begin to move your attention to your belly and notice the weight of your hand there.

Place both hands on your abdomen.

Begin inhaling through your nose, slowly, and imagine that you are completely filling your lungs with air so that the lungs push out your abdomen.

You feel this push on your hands and exhale slowly through your mouth while noticing the movement of the abdomen. Breathe in this manner for a few minutes, inhaling through your nose and exhaling through your mouth and allow your breathing to relax and slow down even more. To simplify it even more: Just be curious about the air reaching the lowest point of your belly. Do this for however long you wish. A few minutes are just fine. However long you decide is just fine.

After you complete the Relaxed Breathing process, tune in to your intuition and ask, "What social groups or people would it be good for me to connect to this week?"

List two to three social groups or specific people you'd like to connect to this week, and when you're going to connect.

WHO: **WHEN:**

I recommend practicing this activity every day for a week or two and watching how the opportunities for social connections grow over that time. You'll find yourself running into people unexpectedly, feeling drawn to ask a colleague to lunch, or responding to emails from friends quicker than you used to. All of these small things will lead to a much bigger connection with your tribe. Of course, you should always trust your intuition to tell you how much practice time would help you.

PRACTICE—
CONNECTING TO YOUR
TRIBE MEDITATION EXERCISE

This is a meditation script to connect you to a like-minded group that also reflects your core inner values and purpose, not just any ol' community. I think of this as your tribe. As you read through this script, set the intention that your inspired self—your inner muse—connects you to a sense of purpose and begins to attract you to your community—

that collaborative community that co-creates a vital and happy life with you.

You're going to practice getting into the vibe of meditating on several options of what a reciprocal community is and how it feels. And you get into a state of fun. The more calm and relaxed you are, the easier it is to receive information. Don't feel pressure to be or do anything.

Just know that whatever you would like to receive from this exercise, you will get at some point. If you don't notice it right away, just keep practicing this exercise until it calls to you.

NOTE: You may find it helpful to slowly read the following script a few times to get used to it, and then read it into an audio recorder to play back for yourself as you stay in a relaxed position. However, you can still learn to reach a relaxed meditative state if you choose to participate with your eyes open (or closed) without recording the script.

Notice your breath for now before you read the script below to help your body get comfortable.

Before we go on this journey, which is like a ride in Disneyland, make sure you're buckled in and you're comfortable. That's what we need to do for this exercise... And to let you know, you're always in control here of what you experience.

Anytime you see or feel something, you can always watch it like a movie... Feeling it like a movie setting. That's one way to experience the process. And if you'd like, you can experience it in full detail... You're always in control... So you can watch or you can be fully in the details of the experience.

To begin, drop into your belly, noticing the sounds around you. Your conscious mind may follow or it may not. Any rustling or any sounds you hear around you will only help to further relax you and help you feel safe...

Whatever happened to you today, getting lost, getting stuck in traffic, being faced with a challenge a work, any stress or tension of your day, any concerns about what will or won't happen... Just exhale those out with the breath. A big exhale.

Practice—Connecting to Your Tribe Meditation Exercise

And feel all the weight of the world dropping off your shoulders down into the center of the earth ... going deeper into the center of your being.

As your conscious mind listens to your breath, going deeper into the center of your being, knowing you're completely safe to do this... Again, breathing into the belly, opening up the belly area, the center of the core... Imagine breathing into the base of your spine, and enlivening that area, knowing this is very healing.

And notice in front of you a clearing with 10 steps, 10 stone steps, and at the base of these steps, a beautiful healing garden where your journey will begin... And there will be a doorway at the base of the steps. With a chair in front of it.

Begin to walk slowly toward those steps, just noticing the detail of the steps themselves, going gently down the top step, the tenth step... Gently down the ninth step... With each step, dropping away more burdens, more conscious concerns.

Letting the conscious mind rest. You can leave it out on a tree branch, imagining it's like a cat. For the next little bit of time, it can sit on the tree branch and just watch... Completely safe to just watch... Or you can set it next to you, putting the cat next to you in this natural place next to the tree stump... And you can let it wait there if you'd like.

To rejoin you at the end of your journey... Going down the eighth step ... now a little more relaxed, releasing down the seventh step...

Imagine counting the steps. Seeing the number seven float by... Relax... Let your conscious mind focus on the number seven... Step down the sixth step, seeing the number six float by...

And maybe even the more you focus on the numbers, the harder they are to see... They just disappear and erase, and they dissolve... Down the fifth step, almost there...

6. Cultivating Collaboration and Tribe

More and more relaxed, more at peace, more at ease... Down the fourth step, down past the third ... down the second... And now you're at the bottom step, noticing the ground beneath your feet.

Noticing more enlivening in your body... Go and find a beautiful flower, in this garden... Maybe your favorite flower, maybe a rose... I don't know, but you have the awareness of which flower you'd like to pick.

So go and pick it, sniffing, inhaling the beautiful scent...

Noticing your breath in the background, relaxing to that... Feeling yourself melt into your body awareness... Go and sit on a seat in the safe garden ... and see or sense a door in front of you ... seeing the color of the door.

Imagine the handle. Is it gold? Silver? Maybe some other color; just notice.

In a moment, you'll go behind that door and visit it—behind this door represents a community that is helpful and reciprocal to you. Count from one to three in just a moment, and when you reach the number three, the door will gently spring open, and you'll go to this place where you feel in pleasant company.

It doesn't matter where or who... Whatever your subconscious mind thinks is best for you to visit, give it the suggestion now to search through the databanks ... gently searching all events you've ever dreamed possible.

Knowing that the infinite exists in all of us, the all possible. Watch your subconscious mind search and find the very best life vision for you to experience now.

Whatever life that is, a life that helps reactivate in you a sense of peace... A sense of purpose... A sense of joy... A sense of pleasure.

Giving yourself permission to have a little more of this flavor in your current daily life, by allowing this reactivation, by visiting this community... You know you'll bring that in more fully to your present day life...

1, letting a little more detail come behind that door...

2, more and more details form, and...

3, so it is, letting the door gently swing open, floating open as you notice it.

Walking over the threshold, noticing whatever details come to you, whatever sounds you hear in the distance. They're there for your own well-being and joy... Noticing colors, maybe colors come to you first.

Noticing body sensations, checking in with your body there, and looking down at your feet as you step over the threshold, making sure the door behind you closes gently, so you can visit this community.

Looking down at your feet in this place, notice if you have shoes, or maybe you're barefoot... Notice the feeling of your feet in this place... Wiggling your toes ... dropping into your belly in this place ... letting that place open ... noticing you're completely safe to do that.

Good. Breathing in, letting that come to you...

Wander through this place more fully, letting your conscious mind follow with your breath ... letting your subconscious mind align all parts of you—unconscious and conscious mind and body. With every breath, they realign for your highest health, healing, and happiness.

Anything you hear in the background helps you to realign for your greatest health, healing, and happiness in community... Allow that to happen now, floating along in this place, along with your breath.

6. Cultivating Collaboration and Tribe

Dropping into that, knowing you're safe ... wrap a beautiful, soft, healing, comforting blanket around you.

Just imagine this blanket is a luminous white, and while you're visiting this place, imagine the sun from this place comes in through the top of your head, a luminous, golden, glowing white... Breathing that in to every cell of your body from the top of your head, down into your forehead, into your cheeks and jaw, and your throat... Into your chest, into your arms, your fingers, your legs, your feet and toes... Good... Letting that luminous, glowing sun clear out anything you're here to release and enliven and activate anything you're here to activate.

Floating along in this place, letting more details come to you at whatever pace is comfortable for you.

Breathing in ... noticing in the distance ... notice who is there in the distance. Walk over to them and say hello... They may feel like a color, or you may see their details completely ... flow with whomever appears.

Notice what they say to you ... any messages they have for you. Just notice ... breathing it in to the heart... You may not hear them verbally... You may see pictures or feel sensations, emotions, breathing into the heart, letting the heart open like a rose.

Taking in whatever messages this person or people have for you... Letting your mind float along, seeing whatever scenes they're there to show you.

Breathing it in ... taking it in.

Let yourself float to ... memories, sensations, emotions that you may need to feel. This will help you activate more feelings of community, happiness, purpose and contentment in this current life.

Take a moment of quiet to just go with whatever comes up in whatever way it comes to you... Just watch and notice... Noticing your breath ... letting yourself be in this place. Imagine a feeling of floating, the more you align with this place... Floating through the scenes of this community.

The pertinent emotions, sensations, and events, may come to you as colors... Or a general awareness... Just notice... Breathing that in...

Now... Ask your subconscious to pick the happiest time, the most joyful time your life... And begin to play it like a scene in your mental movie... Good... Just downloading a movie or picture, imagine you hit the play button... Breathing in, releasing, and relaxing into it.

Just watch the movie after you hit the play button... Notice the main scene that starts to play on that screen... Just sit back and watch... Allow that conscious observer, the protector, to say what it will or filter what it will, but let the movie play.

Take a moment or two to just watch that movie. Just notice.

Just resting in this information, absorbing it, like a sponge... Imagine you're a sponge in the sea ... there to absorb whatever comes your way ... whatever movie is playing; just be curious.

Breathing in from the top of your head into your face, your cheeks, your jaw ... some gold, luminous sunshine into your throat, into your shoulders, down into your chest... Breathing that into the chest cavity, allowing the chest to expand ... breathing in that sparkly gold into the belly, down into the spinal cord, even into the hips.

Down into the legs, all the way down the left leg, opening up to that luminous white light... Down into the right leg, even into the right foot, down into the soles of the feet, down into the left sole, the right sole.

Exhaling, releasing anything you need to release ... down the soles of your feet, as you're watching this movie... Just allow it to play.

If you'd like, you can even imagine you're sitting back in movie theatre seats with popcorn, noticing what scenes come up, who's there, what they say. What do you feel like? Notice the primary emotion in this movie.

You may see it as an observer, or you may have a sensory experience in your belly... A deep knowing that everything is going to be OK... Everything is OK ... everything was OK...

Now, imagine you can leave this place and gently close the door behind you.

Pick another door to visit in the healing garden. A door that represents another community that you could be a part of. Open that door and again just notice what you notice. As you step in and notice this community, it all starts to make more sense... That everything comes in patterns and cycles... An ebb and a flow ... just like the ocean... And that it's all OK. Allowing yourself to float with that for a little while.

Just notice what comes up... Play... Observe.

Breathing that in... Good. Opening up the heart ... being open to community... Just notice.

In a moment or two, you'll need to leave ... this place for now. But know that it's always there in the back of your mind to access at any time... Give yourself another moment or two to take in whatever information you came here to notice.

Just breathe it in... And know that if you're not a naturally visual person, that's OK... You may get the information in a different way... It will come to you kinesthetically, emotionally, auditorially through a message, or as a sensation... A shift in your perception... Just notice throughout the next few days, weeks ... allow whatever information in the next moment or two comes to you... Breathe that in.

Noticing your breath... Noticing how it's slowed through this process, more relaxed... That in and of itself is very healing, to get into relaxed breathing helps reset the nervous system. And yawning is good ... that's a release.

Practice—Connecting to Your Tribe Meditation Exercise

Letting that relaxation wash over you... Feeling more and more relaxed. Imagine that you can float out of that room... Let it recede into the back of your mind for now... Again knowing that it's accessible for you at any time... You may notice it in your dreams if you'd like... However it comes to you, for now, begin to say goodbye to that room. In your mind's eye, find the door that you walked through.

Begin to find that door and open it...

Step through the door into that safe garden, letting the door gently close behind you... Letting the door recede off into the distance... Breathing in... Sitting in that safe garden for a while.

Sitting in that safe garden for a moment or two more.

Allow yourself to notice whatever it is you notice... Breathing that in to your belly, letting it anchor in... Maybe a newfound sense of peace, rediscovered contentment.

As you notice that growing within you, notice it welling up like a blooming flower... Notice what that is... Breathing that in... Good. Taking a deep breath in. Take in a deep feeling of community...

And then whenever you're ready, gently begin to leave that safe garden and walk gently up those ten steps... Up the first bottom step, gently up to the top tenth step, at your own pace...

At your own rate, going up the second, up the third step, and with each step up, bringing more awareness into your present day self.

Releasing anything that you're here to release... Bringing in that new pattern that you're here to activate... Gently bringing in more awareness... Slowly coming up into the room... For several more breaths at your own pace, for the next minute or two... Saying goodbye to those steps whenever you're ready.

6. Cultivating Collaboration and Tribe

Everybody has their own pace that they'll do this at, and that's OK... Letting that recede into the distance... Taking in several more deep breaths, cleansing breaths... Exhaling, releasing.

And whenever you are fully aware, you can begin to open your eyes and stretch. You know that your conscious and unconscious are fully aligned. And you can rub your hands together if you want to help bring you back into the room. And sit quietly for another minute to let everything settle. Have a moment of quiet and deep peace.

This meditation has prepared you to start or continue to build your tribe. Here are some ideas to help you get started:

- Start a potluck in your neighborhood.
- Join a book club.
- Say hello to your next-door neighbor.
- Volunteer to mentor someone.
- Join a group for athletic activities like running or yoga.
- Look online at neighborhood groups like Meetup.com or NextDoor.com.
- Go to a networking event for your industry.
- Join a knitting circle or other hobby group.
- Join a community choir or other community association.

In this chapter, we've learned the value of collaboration and connecting as well as some simple ways to begin that process. In the next chapter, we will explore various roles you choose that connect you to like-minded social groups.

....

KEY TAKE-AWAYS

✓ The first key for this chapter of the book: *appreciate the value of being in a reciprocal community ... of being connected to your tribe. Community means flow.*

✓ The second key for this chapter of the book: *you can do specific meditations to help you build your tribe.*

CHAPTER 7

What Channel Are You On?
Archetypes and Synchronicity

"What makes a modern Wonder Woman? Embracing your goddess within—and not making yourself smaller so that other people can handle you."—Alexandra Schwartz interview of Linda Carter in *Glamour*

This chapter will expand on the notion of the collective unconscious—the set of guiding principles that is passed down in society from generation to generation. These guiding principles are universally present in our individual psyche in the form of archetypes, which are recurring symbols or roles that exist within a society. Archetypes can vary from culture to culture and we can create new archetypes to draw from—ones that empower us. This chapter will explore the unconscious roles that we reference as women in modern society and discuss how we can draw energy from new, emerging archetypes that empower women. It will also introduce the concept of synchronicity—being in the right place at the right time and how applying the correct role in our life can help us synchronize and connect with collaborative people.

Here is the roadmap showing what you will learn in Chapter 7.

- What an Archetype Is and Why It Matters for You

- How to Upgrade Your Archetype App

- Synchronicity and How to Activate It with Archetypes

WHAT AN ARCHETYPE IS
AND WHY IT MATTERS FOR YOU

An archetype is a societally-determined role that embodies a specific way of being. We wear roles or archetypes like clothes. You've probably heard the axiom that everything is a mindset. Mindsets and roles work together and are "wardrobes" or templates for you to "try on" and "wear," so to speak. Our collective culture has developed a closet of outfits for you to start with—each outfit is called an archetype. Each of these archetypes and associated mindsets develops in a number of ways. Sometimes you inherit a mindset from your family, sometimes you pick them up from groups you belong to. But just like any outfit you have in your closet, even though you're used to it, you can still change it. Also, remember if you think of a certain mindset or role as an outfit, you can release the need to get triggered by it and just observe the outfit. You can just look at it and say, "Do I like this outfit or do I want to discard it?" It really is up to you. The reason I taught you alpha state meditation is because it is much easier to clean out your metaphorical closet of outdated roles when you are in your natural relaxed state rather than a keyed-up, reactive state.

It's a little like the following story. My mother-in-law was moving from her home of 30 years into a nice but new place—an assisted living facility. This change was understandably unsettling and I discovered that packing up the things in her closet took forever due to her emotional attachment to the items in the closet. I'd take out an outfit and begin wrapping it up nicely and quickly. However, since the cleaning out of the closet was done while she was in a triggered emotional state, she had a hard time letting outfits go. I'd be packing one of my husband's baby shirts from 1967 and she'd take it from my hand and discuss every aspect of it. I really felt for her during this process. Inside, I was thinking, "I wish we could speed this up because at this rate we'll be here for two years" (and the movers were arriving the next morning). After several hours went by and we'd only packed about five or six items, I decided to take her out for a walk in nature. This helped her get more relaxed and ready for the new transitions, while my niece and nephew packed up the rest of that room. It truly is easy to clean out your metaphorical closet when you have given your mind time to go into an alpha state meditation. Then you can decide as you survey certain archetype or roles whether you want to wear that one, toss it, or donate it to someone else. In a nutshell, an archetype is a role you wear like an outfit. The roles are designed by you and your tribe. You have the choice to change or expand the definition of a role at any time.

The Ladder of Potential

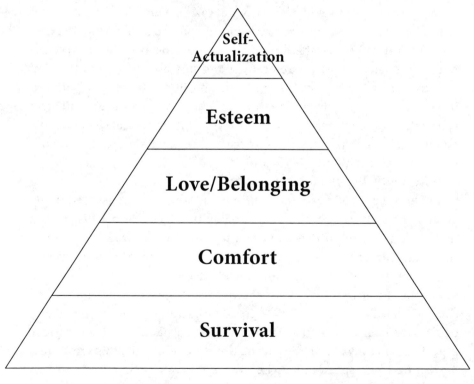

Maslow's Hierarchy of Needs, represented as a pyramid with the more basic needs at the bottom.

You may have heard of the human hierarchy of needs in your high school psychology class. It basically tells us that we are a ladder of potential. The archetypes we are exploring in this book will help you move up the ladder. The various archetypes or roles we wear vary depending on what rung of the ladder of potential we are on.

Are you meeting your full potential? Social research shows that once we as humans meet our basic needs—things like food, water, shelter, and safety—we begin to move toward our self-actualization needs. We reach out to help our fellow human beings. We start to yearn for personal growth, searching for ways to maximize our potential. This idea was first developed by the humanistic psychologist Abraham Maslow.

Humanistic psychologists are interested in the whole person—our needs, desires, and highest hopes. They study how we meet our needs and how our unmet needs impact our behavior. They figure out what makes us healthy people, and how healthy people become exceptional people.

Maslow proposed a universal, global set of needs relating to physiology, safety, self-esteem, and self-actualization. He realized that basic needs, like survival, have to be satisfied in order for people to strive for higher needs like community, connection, and helping others. He felt that all people are eventually compelled to realize their full potential.

The first archetypal outfit we will explore is our Inner Cavewoman. She represents the first rung on the ladder of potential—survival. This is a key archetype to become familiar with as we move from surviving to thriving in life. Since this is one of the most important archetypes in our unconscious and holds thousands of years of memory, we will spend most of our time in this chapter upgrading this archetypal app. Note that our society usually uses the word "caveman" to refer to our early ancestors. For purposes of this book, I will use the term "Cavewoman" to refer to your Inner Cavewoman archetype.

7. What Channel Are You On?

Your Inner Cavewoman Archetype

Thousands of generations back, groups of people, usually about 30 to 60 members, lived together in tribes. Tribes are important in human society. These communities created the "roles" or archetypes that led to the image we currently have of who a Cavewoman was. Research tells us that this Cavewoman went through significant genetic changes that affected who we are as humans today. This research shows that approximately 200,000 years ago, a woman was born with mutations on a gene called FOXP2. These mutations were important because they gave her the ability to understand the concepts of I, me and you, and to understand the concepts of past, present and future. These mutations provided the ability to communicate in abstract language.[1] All of us now have this mutation and it allows us to have amazing abilities like being able to imagine a future positive outcome.

The Cavewoman archetype is important for you because it allows you to access and get in touch with that primal part of you that survived over the eons and got you where you are today. Remember that we have this protective part of our unconscious mind, which has evolved over time to keep us safe. I call this our "Inner Cavewoman." We are the offspring of that extra-vigilant ancestor—a part of our brain evolved to scan the horizon and keep us away from any danger. Our Inner Cavewoman says, "Watch out—don't go." She is only trying to protect us from any remote danger. If it was up to our Inner Cavewoman, she'd just as soon keep you in the cave. But remind yourself that is only one part of your brain. You have to find ways to chat with your Inner Cavewoman and have her meet your Inner Adventurer to learn how life is an adventure to be discovered. Yes, you would avoid many dangers by living in a cave shut away from the world, but would you really want to? I think not. Sometimes, however, if we get stuck in the primal fear of survival, this is where we need to have a little internal chat with our Inner Cavewoman to reassure her that we are safe and can move forward in the modern world and not be fearful of basic concepts such as survival issues.

This archetype asks, "Do I have enough food and water? Am I safe from predators? Have I enough progeny for the species to survive? Am I warm and safe?" These are basic survival needs and the goal is to move on up the ladder of survival to the next level and so on.

The Cavewoman is just starting out on the ladder of potential—the first rung of the ladder, so to speak. Hey, we all gotta start somewhere. The Inner Cavewoman isn't bad—she keeps you from getting hit by a car by telling you to run out of the way to keep out of traffic. But humans created archetypes to help us move up the ladder and not stay stuck; let's visit another archetype, shall we?

The Mom Archetype

As humans evolved, we added many roles to our metaphorical closet. One of the roles that tends to be rife with stereotypes and rigid rules is the Mom archetype. Society tends to load this role with "shoulds" because our Inner Cavewoman wanted her progeny to survive at all costs. At that time, it was all that mattered. There were no careers or vocations to pursue at that time for anyone—males or females. People tended to die at a young age. We did not have the luxury of time to pursue careers, hobbies, or vacations. However, the rules that worked 200,000 ago and attached to this Mom role could probably stand to be updated to meet our present-day reality. As you read through this chapter, I invite you to explore how you would like to personally define the Mom role or archetype (both for yourself if you are a mom and for those in your tribe who are mothers) tailored to your own personal needs and present-day activities. If you feel this archetype needs an update, you can set the intention to update it in the next section on upgrading your archetypal app.

A Note About Male and Female Archetypal Roles

This book at its heart is meant to expand the scope of why women are here and why men are here—and what we understand the default male and female roles to be in present-day life. I want to expand the scope because the unspoken and unconscious scope of the male and female roles are too narrow right now. Let's focus on ways to expand our definition of roles so that we as individuals living in an interconnected web can live happy and fulfilling lives.

As I discussed in prior chapters, there is an inherent balance in nature between two energies—the feminine and the masculine, the yin and yang. The feminine energy is the intuitive part of our brains and generates the wonderful qualities of creativity, collaboration, intuition, and vulnerability. However, our current society tends to overvalue the yang masculine qualities. If we focus only on the yang or masculine energy, that throws our whole system off balance. It's like trying to walk on one leg. Yang energy is represented by the conscious part of our brains. We usually call it the left brain. Masculine or yang energy generates helpful qualities such as focus, individualization, analysis and action. If we ignore the feminine yin qualities and build primarily on a foundation of masculine energy, this marginalizes the feminine yin traits—therefore, we end up with an excess of individualism, competition, analysis, and working.

My work is not meant to diminish the value of masculine energy. In fact, it's quite the opposite. This book is about maintaining the balance in our internal feminine and masculine energy. Research studies show that integrating the feminine traits of intuition, collaboration, and community along with the masculine traits has a transformative effect on both homes and workplaces. When we realize the value of both energies and draw from the best of each, it reinstates a natural balance between the masculine and feminine traits, and empowers us to be our best.

Other Archetypes

There are other role choices that we have developed as we've moved from survival to more advanced rungs of the ladder. As society has more time and resources on its hands, we add roles to our closet. You are probably familiar with an archetypal "Good Girl" or the archetypal "Bad

Girl." There are roles that emulate "the Lover" or "the Intellectual" and everything in between. There are whole volumes that discuss this concept of archetypal roles. We won't go into vast detail here; the point is to realize that these various roles exist. The more you are aware and conscious of the roles, the less they can control you via a knee-jerk unconscious instinct. The more you bring awareness and conscious choice into which outfit or role you will wear, the more you attract helpful circumstances and collaborative people and groups into your daily life. To help you tune in to what types of roles you may wear and help you access the ability to change them at choice or by will, you will learn how to update your archetype app below.

HOW TO UPGRADE ARCHETYPE APPS

To get you ready for the next set of exercises, let's do our quick Body Tune-In exercise. The body is the primary storehouse for all archetype apps. Let's set the intention in this section that your body will begin to acknowledge and release any old apps around archetypes that are outdated and begin to update role apps to a current, present-day version that is most helpful to you.

Preparation—Body Tune-In Exercise

Take a deep breath ... inhale ... and pause for a beat at the top ... now exhale through the mouth, pausing for a beat at the bottom... Do that one more time slowly ... inhale ... and pause for a beat at the top... Now exhale through the mouth, pausing for a beat at the bottom. And one more big deep breath ... inhale ... and pause for a beat at the top... Now exhale through the mouth, pausing for a beat at the bottom. And as you continue, make the exhale a little longer than the inhale...

Continue with these deep breaths, and tune in to your tailbone. Feel the chair holding you, making contact with your muscles. Gently move your tailbone back and forth, feeling that space ground you and center you...

Continue your deep breaths, and move your focus up to your body center, right inside your belly ... feel the muscles in your core contract for a moment ... focus on the strength that it gives your entire body...

As you continue your deep breaths, work your way up toward your rib cage, focus on your solar plexus, which is the spot right between your ribs ... feel it engage while you inhale and exhale ... feel how it helps your breath flow through your body...

And continue to take more deep breaths while you shift your focus to your heart ... concentrate on the lightness you feel deep in your chest ... notice how it rises and falls with every inhale and exhale...

And as you take another deep breath, move your focus to your throat ... sense how the energy in your throat expands as you connect to it ... sense how any blocks you might feel in your communication start to dissipate ... feel the channels of communication start to open and notice your internal voice strengthening...

Continue your deep breaths and now shift your focus up to the spot on your forehead right between your eyes ... feel a lightness fill your body when you focus here ... feel how it clears your mind, relaxes your jaw, and softens your shoulders...

Now take another deep breath and tune in to the point just above your head... Feel a positive current run through your body, a gold-like energy running up and down ... sense how your body lifts and expands, and notice how you stand taller and stretch your spine to touch that point...

Take one more deep breath and imagine yourself connected to all seven points at the same time ... inhale ... and pause for a beat at the top... Now exhale through the mouth, pausing for a beat at the bottom. You are now tuned in to your body. You may even feel lighter and more energized.

Remember, everything is a state of mind. You can regulate and increase this state via your body by tuning into its messages.

Releasing Excess Survival Issues in Your Archetype App

In this section, you are to going to bring a little bit more focus to different areas of the body that store unconscious information. You will have a mental conversation and a calming meditation with these different areas of the body. In so doing, you will help your body upgrade your app move out of the old collective theme of *Survival*. Living in the theme of *Survival* might look like always being afraid of rejection at work, worrying about not having enough, being scared of danger, or having a general anxiousness about what's going to happen.

The body is the primary storehouse for the unconscious. By reading this information and doing the exercises, you move from surviving to **thriving**. This leads to a rich and fulfilling life. By shifting the body's point of reference out of surviving into thriving, your unconscious reflexes reorient and when the unconscious shifts, by definition, the conscious behavior shifts.

One of the areas where the theme of survival is stored is at the base of the tailbone and its connection to the legs. The reflexes stored in that part of the body hold information that helps you survive in the physical world. The legs help you run. For the moment, focus on this area and thank your body for keeping you alive. This is basically your Inner Cavewoman.

Practice—Calming Your Inner Cavewoman Meditation

NOTE: You may find it helpful to slowly read the following script a few times to get used to it, and then read it into an audio recorder to play back for yourself as you stay in a relaxed position. However, you can still learn to reach a relaxed meditative state if you choose to participate with your eyes open (or closed) without recording the script.

To Begin

Bring focus on your legs. They are what ground us and connect us to the earth—our feet and our base, which is at the root of our tailbone. Bring your awareness to your tailbone, and just breathe into the tailbone. Then, I invite you to imagine that you can drop a root down from the base of your tailbone into the earth. Just like you're a tree ... can you imagine? ... drop that root and then release it, because we're going to practice just the concept of feeling that ... and feel how you feel kind of ungrounded when you release the root ... more like you're floating. So now put even bigger roots dropped from the tailbone and imagine it's like the base of a tree ... you know when somebody's sitting on a tree stump in nature. And the roots are really big, like you're sitting on a redwood let's say ... and the roots from your tailbone go all the way down to the earth.

And so then imagine the roots go all the way down past the dirt, past the rocks, past the other trees ... and go into the center of the earth where the earth's magnetic center is. So this is the metaphor for the center of the earth is going to be like the recycling center for any excess survival energy, any tension and any energy you want to release from your body. You know how the trees ... they take our carbon dioxide and they make oxygen. It's a reciprocal cycle. We breathe in oxygen, they breathe in carbon dioxide. So we're going to use this as a metaphor for anything unpleasant you want to release into the earth's magnetic recycling center. Just imagine it melts and it's just like the trees ... that we exhale carbon dioxide and we call that toxic, but the trees breathe in carbon dioxide. So the earth molten center ... takes excess stuff and ... it melts down and it just gets converted into something more useful. It just takes that energy, that emotional energy, and uses it for something else.

So as you exhale, you just release anything anxiety-provoking. And I give you the anecdote about the tree breathing in carbon dioxide because sometimes people originally have this idea like "Why should I put negative emotions into the earth? Is this bad?" No, we're just using it as a metaphor that anything that's carbon dioxide–like for us, the tree will breathe it in and create oxygen.

As you breathe, just release and imagine it's just useful energy anyway. Remember how I said we all survived because we listened to our instincts. Per biology, people that are here today are living because they were afraid of the saber tooth tiger and they ran away. The people who were too mellow and were like "hey dude," they got eaten. So they're not here. Honor your fear and just notice it. Whenever you are ready, your body can release excess concern... It can keep useful body signals for good protection and release excess stuff...

So all this stuff ... in the hips and the legs ... you can visualize any outdated fears release... Any pain, drop down those roots ... down the tree trunk. You can practice, breathe in and exhale and let it drop. And if you feel like you need an even bigger tree trunk, you can practice just dropping the current one you have ... and let it melt away and make it even bigger ... like you're sitting on the biggest redwood ever. And drop any excess stress from the legs. Imagine that drops down in the core to recycle. Any excess tension ... anything you need to let go of that's out of balance for that area.

And when you have that feeling like things are dropping down and releasing, the next thing we're going to add, we're going to bring in some calming, peaceful energy into the feet ... breathe in and imagine energy from the earth coming into the soles of your feet. In eastern medicine, they talk about how walking is good because the way our feet hit the earth generates some useful energy for the feet. So they recommend walking a certain amount of time a day because it actually generates energy in our body.

It's good to put your feet on the earth with no shoes if you are able. Imagine energy coming up through the feet and let's imagine there's a little opening in the soles of the feet where you can breathe in that energy from the earth. And I like to envision a color for the earth energy... Like an earthy color. Bringing that up like a straw up through the feet, up through the legs, into the knees, up into the hips and into the root—the tailbone. Let it bubble up and let it stop there for a while bubbling up ... like you have a fountain of energy bubbling into the knees before it starts shooting up into the hips. And then you can let it bubble up into the hips and stay there for a while before it goes into the tailbone and down back into the earth...

And always give yourself, your subconscious, the suggestions that you drop into your center and you're very relaxed and calm and centered. Your subconscious knows how to do this. Every time it feels the weight of your hands on your legs, it will drop into an even more calm state and you'll just remember how to be in this state. This calm state may wind through the muscles and the nerves, and the joints and the bones, washing away whatever it needs to wash out.

As you work through this meditation, it's helping you realize you're not just a cut-off head looking at the computer; you are a whole body. You may notice that you feel more connected to the earth as you do this meditation more regularly. I encourage you to be out in nature more—spend time on the grass and the dirt. And you may notice when you're in nature it's even easier to experience a relaxed state of mind. Recent research has shown that walking barefoot on the ground helps the body feel relaxed. Just being in nature will help your body to shift from survival to a more engaging and fulfilling sense of being ... to activate a sense of thriving... Return your awareness to the room whenever you feel complete with this meditation.

Talking to Your Inner Cavewoman

After doing the above meditation exercise, let's imagine your Inner Cavewoman is sitting right next to you listening to you read this. OK? As she reads, give her the gentle suggestion that any of those old programs that are too fear based, from way back 100,000+ years ago, she can imagine what it would feel to release those excess fear-based programs out of her body and ask her to feel what present time feels like. Let her know it is a bit safer here in present day. She can play with the concept of having fewer things to worry about. Let her know that you are not going to kick her out. You value how safe she has kept you up to this point. See how relaxed you feel?

After that meditation, you may feel like taking a nap ... that would be fine ... we're going into some deep programming. This is ancient programming that ran your ancestors ... the genetic memory to run from the saber-toothed tiger, and to store up extra fat and all of those related Cavewoman programs.

Now, you and your Inner Cavewoman can just notice and be aware of these programs. You can ask your unconscious mind; do I really need to be so vigilant about a saber-toothed tiger these days? Do I really need to worry so much about my life goals? While you are reading this, a part of you knows that we all went through feast and famine 100,000 years ago, right? You found the nuts and berries then and you chowed down on whatever you could find because you had to fatten up. Nowadays, we have a mini-mart on every corner, so you don't need that as much as we did in the past. So all that old programming that tells you to scrounge and store—let's image we give the body a suggestion to clear that out just a bit and relax. These are all survival issues from the distant past. Realize they were helpful at that time. It is time to move from survival to thriving.

7. What Channel Are You On?

Moving from Survival to Comfort

Since we've been focusing on survival issues, let's imagine we're moving up the ladder of needs to comfort issues. We are upgrading your archetype app to notice and integrate the feeling of comfort in your daily life. In the next section, we will do this same process to move from comfort up to the belonging rung of the ladder.

We are going to tailor the *Focus Words* tool (from Chapter 5) to help you move into a feeling of comfort. Remember, in this exercise you focus on a word to help you reach a relaxed alpha state. You need approximately five minutes for this exercise. However, don't worry about timing it for exactly five minutes. Just flow with it and finish when you feel complete.

Read through the exercise once and then practice it with your eyes open or closed.

The Focus Word is **Comfort.**

Be gentle with yourself. There is no right or wrong here. If other thoughts pop into your head during this process, let them go. Let them float off like clouds. You can keep your eyes open or closed for this exercise.

Begin to repeat your focus word, Comfort. You can say it out loud or in your mind.

Say your focus word… Comfort.

Comfort… Keep gently repeating the word "Comfort."

Comfort … allow a sense of comfort to wash over you…

Comfort, where do you feel it in your body… Notice… Be curious…

Continue with your focus on the word Comfort for a minute or two more… However long it feels right to you … and then return your full attention to the room. Open your eyes if they were closed.

Moving from Comfort to Belonging and Beyond

In this section, we will do this same process to move from comfort to the belonging rung of the ladder. We are upgrading your archetype app to notice and integrate the feeling of belonging in your daily life. Some of you may have already reached a sense of integration with this rung of daily needs; however a little revisiting of the feeling of belonging never hurts. As your unconscious upgrades its archetype app, it may automatically move up to the levels above Comfort, Belonging, and Self-Esteem. This process is not really linear, it is holistic. This process also helps you update any roles on each level that may be out of date for you. This process activates the intuitive mind, as you may remember from Chapter 1 accessing the feminine yin side of human nature—which is intuitive and sees the whole picture, not just the linear way of being. The intuitive mind automatically knows which archetypes to update, just like when you press the "update this app?" button on your phone.

We are going to tailor the *Focus Words* tool (from Chapter 5) to help you move into a feeling of belonging. Remember, in this exercise you focus on a word to help you reach a relaxed alpha state. You need approximately five minutes for this exercise. However, don't worry about timing it for exactly five minutes. Just flow with it and finish when you feel complete.

Read through the exercise once and then practice it with your eyes open or closed.

The Focus Word is **Belonging**.

Be gentle with yourself. There is no right or wrong here. If other thoughts pop into your head during this process, let them go. Let them float off like clouds. You can keep your eyes open or closed for this exercise.

Begin to repeat your focus word, **Belonging**. You can say it out loud or in your mind.

Say your focus word... Belonging.

Belonging... Keep gently repeating the word "Belonging."

Belonging … allow a sense of belonging to wash over you…

Belonging, where do you feel it in your body… Notice… Be curious…

Continue with your focus on the word "Belonging" for a minute or two more, however long it feels right to you, and then return your full attention to the room. Open your eyes if they were closed.

Completing the App Update

We have completed a few activities to update a few of your role apps. In this section, choose a specific role that you would like to explore and update to work better for you. Remember, the roles we wear also affect how we connect to our tribe and how we implement our life vision. In this activity, you will achieve a neutral mindset toward that role by using the tool we learned earlier called Relaxed Breathing.

This can be done while sitting in a chair or lying down, whichever you prefer. However, your breathing pattern is most noticeable when you are lying down. Get as comfortable as you would like before starting this exercise. You'll need at least five minutes of uninterrupted time for this exercise. Have a specific role in mind as you read through this.

- Place one hand on your upper chest and the other hand on your belly, near your waistline.

- Breathe at your normal pace and notice which hand rises and falls most noticeably.

- If you notice that you are breathing mostly into your chest, use your breath to push out the hand on your belly. Inhale through your nose and exhale through your mouth while you notice the rise and fall of your abdomen. Now place both hands on your belly.

- As you notice your breath, think about a role that you'd like to be more neutral about. You may even wish to shift how you act in this role. Picture the role in your mind's eye as a specific outfit you wear or as a specific color and place it about a foot outside your body as you think about it. Notice your breath and breathe into your belly, the belly gently rising and falling with each breath. Notice the situation outside of you and then bring your attention back to your breath. You may notice that the role seems different as you place it outside of your physical space. Keep your focus on your breathing pattern as you leave the role outside of your mental and physical space for the next couple of minutes.

Continue focusing on your breath for a few minutes... Bring your awareness back into the room when you are ready.

At this point, you can consciously decide if you would like to keep the role, or if you would like to keep it but update it, say, the color of the outfit changes to adapt to your personality. Just allow your unconscious mind to pick a calming color and notice the shift. If you are not visual just set the intention that it shifts for you. After you set the intention, you have completed the exercise.

SYNCHRONICITY AND HOW TO ACTIVATE IT WITH ARCHETYPES

Certain older archetypes come with a pre-set bunch of mindsets. The pre-set bunch of archetype mindsets are like the apps that come pre-programmed in our phones—the ones that take up space and battery, but we don't ever really use. They may have been helpful to push us forward when we were Cavewomen collecting nuts and berries. If we felt "life was a struggle," we, as those Cavewomen, just persevered and assumed a struggle to collect enough nuts and berries or whatever to feed our offspring, this mindset may have given us motivation at that time to scrabble for what we needed to survive. As we moved up the ladder of human potential and learned how to efficiently raise and store food, that learned mindset from the Inner Cavewoman of "life was a struggle" became maladaptive to keep in our unconscious program. Life became easier to live as we discovered more efficient tools. Mindsets we hold (whether consciously chosen or pre-programmed in our subconscious from the collective unconscious) draw people and situations to us. These mindsets are the foundation of synchronicity, which I define as basically being in the right place at the right time.

Synchronicity Mindsets

Here are a few common mindset traps that people tend to fall into. See if you can notice them more consciously in your own life.

- The life is a struggle mindset.

- The I'm so busy mindset.

- The I'm better than so-and-so at _____ mindset.

- The poor me mindset.

- The parenting mindset—run kids to endless soccer and have no adult personal identity.

Here's a recent story from my own life about my mindset and synchronicity.

I'm learning to wear the mindset of *life brings me what I need*. For example, I was meditating on what I wanted to create and I visualized a small-town vibe where I would run into people I know and love often. I live in large city that is growing too fast and was feeling lonely and disconnected from community at the time.

In meditation I asked, "(Unconscious) show me where I go to find this."

Two days later, I was going to a new acupuncturist. As I walked out of the office at the end of my appointment, my neighbor was walking in! That night at a restaurant for dinner, I saw my new web designer with his sister, who is a teacher at my daughter's school! The world brought me lots of synchronicities.

Take a few minutes and think about it ... what mindsets or roles do you find yourself wearing? Notice which ones help you and which ones hold you back. We will do an exercise later in this chapter to clarify the helpful ones for you while removing a few of the unhelpful ones.

Let's talk a bit about how your mindsets relate to synchronicity. First, it's important to know that synchronicity is a very powerful concept and tool to help you navigate life with more flow and create what you want out of life. It helps you create the life of your dreams, whether that's a beautiful soul mate or a wonderful, innovative company.

For purposes of this book, "Synchronicity is a concept, first introduced by analytical psychologist Carl Jung, which holds that events are 'meaningful coincidences' if they occur with no causal relationship yet seem to be meaningfully related."[2]

For instance, you've been thinking about a friend you haven't seen in six months and then, suddenly, you run into her in the grocery store. Or your washing machine breaks and you need to buy a new one. Out of the blue, your neighbor says, "I'm getting a new washing machine and need to get rid of my old one. Any chance you want it?" What I want you to learn from this is that things you need can literally fall into your lap if you have your mental filters set helpfully. You don't have to agonize over it. It can just come to you. And that's one way synchronicity shows up in life.

There are many theories on how this works. Many meditation teachers say that by being in the meditative state, you will have more synchronicity happen. For simplicity, let's think of it this way. Synchronicity works because we are part of a collective unconscious.

What you believe draws people and situations to you. Therefore, for synchronicity to flow the best, it's important for you to hold mind-sets or archetypes that reflect what you want, not what you don't want. In other words, synchronicity will reflect the mindsets you choose.

To keep it simple to apply, I'd love for you to practice this mindset this week: *Life brings me what I need.*

Say the phrase "Life brings me what I need" first thing in the morning when you wake up. Try it for a week and every time you say it feel the sensation of receiving something you need. Since we are calming down our Inner Cavewoman, let's keep it simple and notice every time we eat, life brings us what we need. Notice how that feels when you eat throughout that week.

Now that you've read some examples of mindsets, think about some synchronicities that have shown up in your life recently.

Get Clear on What You Want

Recall that synchronicity is the acausal connection between two or more seemingly unrelated events. For instance, your boss wants you to put together a presentation on a topic you're not familiar with. That afternoon, you check LinkedIn and see an article on that exact topic, written by an expert in the field. Voila—it's the perfect article to help you get started on your work! It works in this example because the person is clear about what she wants (an article on a certain topic).

But I know that sometimes, even when you think you have clarity, synchronicity still doesn't show up … that's usually because two things you desire are in conflict. Being clear on what you want is necessary so that you don't have two conflicting values! What does that mean? Well, here's an example:

Let's say you want to create an empire of real estate properties to manage for residual income, but you also value freedom and the ability to travel at the drop of a hat—your subconscious probably is going to feel stuck on creating that because managing properties means you have to be around at a moment's notice if your tenants' toilet clogs or the water heater breaks. So to create both, you need a solution—how do I keep my ability to travel yet have residual income from real estate?

One value that's important to you is the belief "I value freedom" and on the other side "I value residual income." If those two values clash, synchronicity will have a hard time activating in your mental filter. So you have to visualize a third concept that acts as a bridge between the two values—"I can have someone manage the property so I can still get residual income and travel at the same time." Just because you have two conflicting value sets doesn't mean that synchronicity can't happen. You just have to find a bridge to connect the two!

If you find yourself facing two conflicting values or synchronicity isn't showing up for you, here are some simple questions to help you build a bridge like in the example above. A good place to start is exploring who you are.

- What defines you?
- What is important to you?
- What do you value?

These three questions will help you find clarity and identify a bridge (or two or three!) that can connect any conflicting values you may have. I encourage you to really get clear on what you want in life. That is the key to unleash this flow that will help you create the life of your dreams. With synchronicity, clarity is key and allows synchronicity to flow into your life! And, when you define what you value, it's easier to connect via synchronicity with the communities you resonate with.

Think about or journal on these three questions to help synchronicity flow to you and see what happens.

Jung's development of this concept of synchronicity came to him in an interesting scenario. He was working through a mental impasse with one of his clients. Her over-analysis of her life was holding her back from accessing unconscious material that would help her overcome her problems. One night, the client dreamed about receiving a necklace with a golden scarab on it. The scarab was very rare—a *cetonia aurata*. The next day, during their session, an insect flew into Jung's window. Jung caught it and discovered, surprisingly, that it was a golden scarab, a very rare presence for that climate and area. He handed it to the client and said, "Here is your scarab." Synchronicity is about meaningful coincidence. In Jung's case with his client, the meaningful coincidence was between the scarab in the dream the night before and its appearance in real life, in his office.

Notice that this coincidence is not senseless, a simple coincidence. Jung realized the scarab's archetypal association with death and rebirth. The client, through this process, experiences a "death" of the over-analytic, "worrier" part of her personality, which was causing her block transformation, and a rebirth and revitalization of the helpful parts of her persona. Thus, a significant coincidence that is acausally connected helped her lead a happier life.

Synchronicity is a powerful concept, which is why I want to make sure you understand it 100 percent. Here's another example of synchronicity from my own life.

My Own Story of Synchronicity

Synchronicity happens to me a lot. My best memory is from a few years ago. I had taken about four years off from work to raise my daughter. My husband had been working at the same good and reliable job for years, but he was burnt out and needed a break. I wracked my left brain for a way for him to take an unpaid four-month sabbatical from work and for us to be able to pay for living expenses while we went on the road.

I talked to a tax accountant about possibly taking an early high-penalty withdrawal from my IRA. He thought I was a nutty hippie. We figured we needed about $60,000 to pull off the sabbatical, get a small RV, and see the country during his sabbatical. This is something we'd dreamed of doing before my daughter started school and I went back to running a business.

Then I decided I'd try the meditation route instead of the left brain route to get to the best solution. I meditated and pictured having the $60,000.

Through a series of coincidences or synchronicity, one week later, a check for $60,000 came to me in the mail—the exact amount we had needed in order to complete our dream!

I think if we all learn how to consciously activate synchronicity (and it is a learnable skill), it will revitalize our lives as well as our surrounding communities and our lives will become easier. Imagine the impact it can have on our society then. When you are doing well, the surrounding community does well too. I believe that synchronicity points to the fact that we are all connected—let's connect in a spirit of sharing and cooperation, shall we?

PRACTICE— ANOTHER WAY TO UPDATE YOUR ARCHETYPAL APP

Sometimes we get stuck on one outfit that we may have inherited, so to speak, from an ancestor or family member. For example, Sabrina (from the last chapter) had hit a roadblock. She had learned to boil down her life vision to something focused, and she learned some basic exercises to easily be in a relaxed alpha state. She did the exercises regularly for a couple of weeks and also worked on developing some action steps and community. But part of her was feeling stuck. I introduced her to the idea of her Inner Cavewoman, synchronicity and flow, and how upgrading her app to a more current one would help her life flow.

She agreed that this idea could hold the key to change and help her remove the roadblock she faced. As we worked together, I asked her what could be one attitude or belief she may have that could be blocking her from creating a happy work-life balance. She had wanted more opportunities for advancement as well as more work-life balance. Before we started working together, she was feeling shut down on reaching work-life balance and her life vision, so we did a few of the alpha state meditation processes on updating her archetypal app. In doing these exercises, her Inner Cavewoman archetype said the limiting belief was "Life has to be hard." And going through this process, she actually felt generations of hard labor, hunger, and struggle stored in her body memory. As we completed the process, she asked her Inner Cavewoman to release the "Life has to be hard" mindset and update it to something more useful for the present time. She observed her Inner Cavewoman removing it and updating it to "Life can flow." Now you can practice too.

Let's go into alpha state.

If you are able, lie comfortably on the floor, place one hand on your upper chest and the other hand on your belly.

For now, breathe how you normally would and notice which hand rises and falls the most.

If you are currently tense or anxious, you tend to breathe from the chest with short, shallow breaths.

If you notice that you are breathing from the chest, begin to move your attention to your belly and notice the weight of your hand there.

Place both hands on your abdomen.

Begin inhaling through your nose, slowly, and imagine that you are completely filling your lungs with air so that the lungs push out your abdomen.

You feel this push on your hands and exhale slowly through your mouth while noticing the movement of the abdomen. Breathe in this manner for a few minutes, inhaling through your nose and exhaling through your mouth and allow your breathing to relax and slow down even more. To simplify it even more: Just be curious about the air reaching the lowest point of your belly.

As you tune in to your breath, you see your Inner Cavewoman in the distance. You walk toward her ... feel your feet on the grass. You go say hello to your Inner Cavewoman. At this point, ask her gently, "Can you please remove the mindset 'Life is a struggle' in my current app and install 'Life flows a bit easier'"—notice what she does and how she reacts, reassure her she is safe in this present time...

Do this interaction for however long you wish. You can chat with her a bit or just a few minutes is fine too. As you imagine a shift and when you feel ready, you can return your full attention to the room.

Here you were introduced to some very powerful tools. They are very powerful concepts and techniques to help you navigate life with more flow and create what you want out of life. It helps you create a more balanced and happy life.

New Emerging Archetypes

After this brief overview of a few common archetypes, I invite you to play with the notion that you can mix and match archetypes and make up new ones that work for you effectively for the modern era.

What would your own personalized archetype look like or act like?
You can design new archetypes. The average person can now design apps to put on his or her phone. It is the same concept. Design your role in a way that works for you.

In this chapter, you have learned how you can choose roles that work for you and upgrade your roles to be more useful to this present day. You have learned to calm your Inner Cavewoman too so that you can be more present. You also learned ways to be in the right place at the right time.

••

Key Take-Aways

✓ The first key for this chapter of the book: *archetypes are chosen roles.*

✓ The second key for this chapter of the book: *you can update your archetypes at any time.*

References

1. Witt, K. (2016). *Shadow light: Illuminations at the edge of darkness.* Tucson: Integral Publishers.
2. Synchronicity. (n.d.). In *Wikipedia*. Retrieved from https://en.wikipedia.org/wiki/Synchronicity.

CHAPTER 8

Higher Mind States—
Neutrality as a Tool

"The world will be saved by the western woman."—The Dalai Lama
at the Vancouver Peace Summit 2009

Acting neutrally is the ability to take excess emotion out of your response to a person, an archetype or role, or to a situation so you can act in the most fair, reasonable manner. It is also realizing that a situation or a person's behavior usually isn't about you personally. Most of the time people are not reacting to you as much as they are reacting to their internal world. Remember that a reaction is from the subconscious. You achieve more optimal results in work and life when you act rather than react. Learning the neutrality tools in this chapter will help you achieve your goal more effectively. I will help you explore how you react in an example scenario and see how changing your perspective can change your response to a situation.

If you are neutral or relatively non-emotional, it's more likely that you'll react in a positive way rather than having a damaging or unhelpful reaction because you won't have an emotional attachment to the outcome. This chapter will teach key tools to help you remain neutral in challenging situations and will help you better listen to your gut hunches and therefore end up being at the right place at the right time more often.

Here is the roadmap showing what you will learn in Chapter 8.

- The Neutrality Tool

- Neutrality in Action—New Perspectives

- Flip the Switch

- Remaining Neutral

- The Landing Pad—A Tool for Taking Excess Emotion Out of Work Tasks

- Focused Attention as a Neutrality Tool

THE NEUTRALITY TOOL

In this chapter, you're going to learn an important tool vital to reaching your life vision and goals—the tool of neutrality. Acting neutrally is the ability to take excess emotion out of your response to a person or to a situation so you can act in the most fair, reasonable manner. It is also realizing that the situation or the person's behavior isn't usually about you. Most of the time people are not reacting to you as much as they are reacting to their internal world. Remember that a reaction is from the subconscious. You achieve more optimal results in work and business when you act rather than react. Learning the neutrality tools in this chapter will help you achieve your work goal more effectively by keeping you on your path. It will help you explore how you react in an example scenario and see how changing your perspective can change your response to the situation.

To Explore

Imagine you are in a meeting discussing the budget and other details for a new product. One of the meeting attendees, Lewis, is unhappy and is getting quite angry with you because you suggested that the product be reduced in scope. While you're explaining that the marketing research doesn't support the expected revenues contained in the original proposal, you're constantly being interrupted by Lewis. He is preventing you from presenting your ideas and suggestions, and he seems irritable with you.

Take a few moments to answer the following questions.

1. How would you feel in this situation (you can imagine being in a similar situation in the past), and what emotions come up?

2. Where do you feel this in your *body*? (Note the *first* place that pops into your awareness.)

3. What sensations do you notice in your *body*?

In this situation, you might react to his behavior by raising your voice, clenching your jaw, and getting irritated. Or you can learn to become more emotionally neutral by learning not to absorb other people's negativity.

NEUTRALITY IN ACTION— NEW PERSPECTIVES

Let's imagine that later, you find out that Lewis wrote the original proposal for the project. He's not very experienced in conducting the numerical research and used assumptions in his proposal in place of actual data. It was his first product proposal and he was worried that if the project were reduced in size, his ideas wouldn't be taken seriously again. This caused him to act defensively. He wasn't trying to irritate you—he was trying to protect his own position in the company. He wasn't really mad at you at all.

It turns out that he was acting out of a self-protection pattern.

Initially you may have felt stressed, but after understanding why

Lewis is being irritable, you may notice you have a different emotional response and your body sensations may be different.

Take a few moments to answer the following questions below:

1. How do you feel about this situation now that you have this new perspective?

2. What emotions are you experiencing with this new information?

3. Where do you feel this in your *body*?

4. What sensations arise in your *body*?

Compare what you wrote down in your initial thoughts about Lewis to your thoughts after you had a new perspective.

FLIP THE SWITCH

In the last exercise we discussed the difference a change in perspective can have in our reactions. Now, let's practice with a simple example of a situation where we are emotionally unattached or neutral.

Think of a time when you flipped the switch to turn on your kitchen light and it didn't work. Did you get excessively angry at your light? Probably not. Did you take it personally, thinking the light switch was purposely trying to irritate you? Probably not.

Why are we more neutral in the situation with the kitchen light? Usually in these types of situations, you take action: you unscrew the light bulb associated with the switch and you replace it with a new one and try the light switch again. Here you take action to resolve the issue without feeling personally invested in the issue or the event. You usually don't waste time thinking that the light is out to irritate you. Sure, you might get annoyed for an instant, but you don't let yourself get tangled in any emotions for too long.

Flip the Switch

When you think of the example of the light switch not working:

- Do you feel a reaction in your body?

- Is this feeling different than in the Lewis example from the previous exercise?

- Did you feel it somewhere different?

- Did you feel as frustrated as you did with Lewis?

When you have an emotional reaction to a person or event, it is partly because you store a physical trigger to that person in your body. You store that thought or reaction in your body—for instance, your gut churns.

If you are neutral or relatively non-emotional—like in the above example—it is more likely that you won't feel that acutely or at all, or store it in your body because you don't have an emotional attachment to it. You usually see things like the light switch as something outside of your body, external to you. You can use the same concept with people or events to help you remain more relaxed and neutral. It is a key tool to learn for increased happiness in your daily life and reaching your goals.

If, instead of reacting to Lewis, you kept the event external—you could see the issue as outside of you—you could then take action to resolve it in a more calm and relaxed manner. Perhaps you'd ask Lewis if he would like to say something and then let him speak, so he doesn't feel the need to keep interrupting you. Maybe you'd explore the following.

- Am I taking this personally and assuming Lewis is trying to irritate me?

- Or maybe Lewis is reacting to his internal triggers? (Consider what his triggers might be.)

When a potentially stressful or irritating event or interaction happens, remember the concept of a light switch as a symbol of a neutrality building tool.

REMAINING NEUTRAL

Remember the example about Lewis we used in the Neutrality Tool. Think of a situation from your life that is similar to that example. Picture the situation in your mind and choose a symbol or image to represent it. For example, you could picture Lewis' face or a meeting room at work. Got your picture? Now do the following.

- Close your eyes and scan your body for a moment.

- Notice where you hold any emotional reaction to that situation in your body.

- Imagine placing that reaction outside of your body. Do this by placing the picture you chose to represent it, Lewis' face, for instance, outside of your body.

- Notice how you feel when you place the situation outside of your body.

- Switch back and forth, visualizing the image inside your body and then outside your body. Practice this for a few moments.

- Notice how you feel.

Next, hold a picture of a light switch in your mind. Imagine that you replace your picture from the above exercise with the light switch picture. In other words, make your situation become like the light switch. Then visualize it outside of you about a foot away. How do you feel now?

Most people notice that they begin to feel more neutral when they do this neutrality process. In what situations do you feel most able to reach a neutral mindset? Think of at least one.

Take a minute to write down your situation(s). Why do you feel more neutral in those situations?

Now think about how you can take these neutral feelings and apply them to situations where you feel triggered.

Being aware of what triggers you to feel upset in a situation and in what situations you naturally feel more neutral enables your subconscious to recognize what makes you feel neutral. In this way, you can more easily access that feeling when you're in potentially upsetting situations. You can train your body to have a calmer, more neutral response to your old triggers.

What types of strengths and positive behaviors are you using in potentially stressful situations where you practice neutrality? Write down at least one strength or positive behavior below.

THE LANDING PAD

You just learned a process called Remaining Neutral. When you learn how to remain neutral, you easily align with others and create win-win relationships. Practicing neutrality by remembering your strengths and positive behaviors will expand your horizons and enable you to discover more effective ways of dealing with potentially uncomfortable situations.

Imagine the following scenario. You receive an email from one of your colleagues—let's say her name is Amanda. Her email is long and dramatic, detailing how she has had a rough weekend. Her father is in the hospital so she hasn't had much sleep and is behind on a project that you are both involved in. She's requesting that you take up some slack for her on the project. You've heard stories that she has a lot of drama in her life and that she has a tendency to pull others into her dramas, causing them to get lost in the overwhelming emotion. Instead of helping Amanda, her empathetic colleagues and friends mean well, but they end up getting pulled down by the emotions of her story. Because of the drama pattern she tends to fuel, no one gets much done and people around her are affected by her sense of being overwhelmed.

Think about what you should do in this scenario. Can you be an empathetic, caring person, but not get emotionally drained by Amanda's problems? Yes, you can! There are certain philosophies that teach us how to cope and process emotions by being a "neutral witness" to a situation. This is achieved by becoming and remaining neutral to potentially emotionally draining situations. Instead of getting personally involved you practice not getting emotional in the situation. This will help prevent the situation from sapping your emotional energy. We will practice one of these neutrality tools now.

The Landing Pad: Visualization Activity

Imagine that you are reading the dramatic and emotional email from Amanda.

- What emotions come up for you? For example, sadness, stress, or irritation.

- Give your emotions a color and/or a shape. For this example, pretend that they are fiery red fishing hooks that are shooting toward you, trying to pull you into the story.

- Instead of letting the hooks land on you, imagine that you have a landing pad in front of you, a neutral place for the emotional hooks to land. This will prevent you from internalizing the situation and becoming emotionally invested in it. You can empathize with Amanda and take the role of a colleague or friend who understands that we all experience good times and difficult ones.

- However, you can keep Amanda's situation and emotions external to you. In doing this, you are practicing neutrality; this will enable you to make clear, logical decisions about the best course of action for both you and Amanda.

Spend a few more moments imagining you are reading Amanda's email, and "watch" or sense the emotional hooks landing on the pad in front of you. Move the landing pad out so it is about a foot in front of you. Then, after you've finished reading the email and you have all the drama and hooks on your landing pad, move the landing pad further away from you, into an empty place, and let it float away. Imagine that it disappears into thin air, or gets washed away to the sea, or some other image that helps you to clear it out of your mind and free up your mental space.

- Then imagine saying "Hello" to Amanda wherever she is now. Take a few moments to imagine talking to her and acknowledging that her situation must be quite difficult; say whatever else you want to communicate to her.

- Now imagine you say "Goodbye" to her and say whatever you need to say so that you are able to let it go. You can use this process for any emotion-provoking situation that comes up in your life; it's especially useful for dealing with emails like this.

To help build and strengthen your neutrality skills, ask yourself the following questions.

- Is it your responsibility to solve Amanda's problems?
- Should this be your role?
- What is one way you could be empathetic but neutral for Amanda? (Hint: the exercise above.)
- What is best for you and what is best for Amanda?
- If you tend to get very emotional in others' situations, why do you think that is?

Use the landing pad technique and these questions any time you feel you're in danger of internalizing someone else's problems. This way you'll be able to empathize with situations like Amanda's while remaining neutral enough to help support her in more useful ways that don't cause excessive drama and distract you from your goals.

You have learned a few exercises on how to remain neutral when triggered. If, after going through the questions from the last exercise, you still feel a need or pull to worry for someone or something, set a timer for five minutes. Spend that time literally worrying for that specific issue in all possible imagined scenarios. Put all your attention on whatever you are worried or stressed about for the whole five minutes. Then, when the timer stops, distract yourself with some other task or activity. Get up and go do that other task. Giving yourself five minutes will help get it out of your system, and it will be easier to let go. It is an amazingly simple technique, and it works.

If you do the timer activity, I suggest you wind down and bring in a calming feeling by doing a simple meditation such as the Relaxed Breathing meditation.

Get as comfortable as you would like and give yourself about five minutes of uninterrupted time to complete this process.

- Place one hand on your upper chest and the other hand on your belly.

- Breathe at your normal pace and notice which hand rises and falls most noticeably.

- If you notice that you are breathing mostly into your chest, use your breath to push out the hand on your belly. Inhale through your nose and exhale through your mouth while you notice the rise and fall of your abdomen. Now place both hands on your belly.

- If you are having difficulty being aware of this area, then place a small book on your abdomen and notice the book rise and fall as you breathe (lying down). Take a few moments to just notice the rise and fall of your belly with the weight of the book there … gently rising and falling with the breath, gently breathing in and out…

- Notice your breath and breathe into your belly, the belly gently rising and falling with each breath…

Continue focusing on your breath for a few minutes… Bring your awareness back into the room when you are ready and allow yourself to feel relaxed and revitalized.

The Landing Pad

In this chapter, you learned several exercises in which you took an internal emotional reaction to a situation and neutralized it. These neutrality tools are here to help you optimize your responses to life's challenges, stay on your life path, and continue to experience ease and flow as you create the life of your dreams.

••

KEY TAKE-AWAYS

✓ The first key for this chapter of the book: *remaining neutral doesn't mean ignoring your emotions. It means choosing not to be reactive. Continue to stay on your chosen path.*

✓ The second key for this chapter of the book: *staying in neutrality is a choice you can make daily, and the more you practice it the easier it will be!*

Epilogue

You did it! You are now at the end of this book. You have learned a five-step process to a happier, more balanced life. Let's do a quick review:

1. **DEFINE**—*You Uncovered Your Goals for Your Life:* You learned to craft a short phrase to **define** and "feel" your desired life vision—your goal—in the present tense. You learned this in Chapter 1. For example, "I have enjoyable work and supportive relationships" or "I find joy in work and life."

2. **VISION**—*You Accessed Your Natural In-Born Relaxed Alpha State:* You learned to get into a relaxed "alpha" meditative state to help propel you to your life **vision**. You learned this in Chapters 2 and 3. Pick any of the guided meditations that resonate with you and practice one in order to reach that alpha state and build your intuitive insights in daily life. I have included several of the guided meditations, along with some new ones, in Appendix A so that you have them as a handy resource and can access them readily.

3. **ACT**—*You Took Action:* Continue to **follow any action steps** or **insights** you get while in the relaxed alpha state to own your power and move into your life vision. You learned this in Chapters 4 and 5.

4. **CONNECT**—*You Started to Cultivate a Collaborative Community:* You cultivated a **community** that is reciprocal and collaborative and chose the role you play in that community.

Epilogue

I encourage you to continue to cultivate this community. You learned this in Chapters 6 and 7.

5. **NEUTRALIZE**—*You Learned to Use Neutrality to Create Change in Your Life:* Applying the skill of **neutrality** helps you stay on your path. You learned this in Chapter 8.

I invite you to continue to apply these principles and tools to your daily life to make it even more wonderful. I hope you have enjoyed this journey in reading this book. I know it may sound odd, but I really do care for you and care that you have an enjoyable and prosperous life filled with wonderful events and memories. Learn to own your power.

Just be happy. Find your interconnected tribe. Do what *you* want to do. Connect with whatever your heart feels is your purpose and *do* that—whether it's work and have kids or take a sabbatical and have kids, or don't have kids, or travel the world, or be a nomad, or whatever combination you decide. Release the need to have outside approval for these actions. Have the courage to let go of oppressive expectations and just do what consciously aligns to your highest aspirations. Find your way to do good in the world and do it.

Own your power.

Appendix A.
Some New and Review
Guided Meditations for Step 2
of the Muse Process

THE NEW YOU GUIDED MEDITATION

If you like variety, here is a new meditation for you. It is also a bit longer than some of the other meditations you learned in the book. In this meditation, you'll be envisioning and imagining visiting your future, your new life, the one that's being created even now, and then coming back to the present in order to integrate it happily.

The thing with this meditation is that our mental space gives us permission in the future to do whatever we want, in whatever way we want to. Sometimes, if we get caught too much in the distant or recent past, we begin to think we are stuck or set in a pattern and feel it can be hard to break out of it. Right? And so the point of practicing the future visit is to learn ways to create something different—a new pattern.

Because if it was all perfect, if it was all going exactly the way you wanted, you probably wouldn't be choosing to do this meditation. There is an exception, situations where people are philanthropic—they've gotten what they wanted in life and they're exactly where they want to be. Then, they're using the power of their imagination and their creativity to create a future for the world at large, for their fellow human beings, and other critters—not just human beings, but the whole planet. So, if you want to use your energy for that too, you'll find suggestions in the meditation to create a wonderful future for the world at large, not just for ourselves, but for those around us. Research has shown that if we are happy, the people around us, even if they don't know us, are happier too.

Part of my mission in life is to give people tools, whether in books or in person, to be happy and successful. You can have enlightened self-interest—because if we're getting happier, and other people are getting happier, it's a reciprocal effect, and everyone is happier. Make sense? We want to live in this kind of cosmic soup of happiness. Not misery. If people are miserable around you, you resonate with the misery, and we don't want that, right? I am offering tools to make it easier for us to be happy and peaceful.

Basically, as acupuncture philosophy showed you earlier in the book, we are electromagnetic, and we create from our thoughts. I have a framed quote in my office lobby from Confucius: "Every thought you think is generating your future, and every action you do is generating your future." Thoughts and actions are tied together. Whatever we are thinking, we are usually doing. We're going to work with the power of our thought to create our future. The future is not set in stone, there's no fate. Let's enjoy the process of planting the seeds. It's kind of like a video game. Imagine that there are all these possibilities programmed in to your life app or program. If you go to the left, this happens. If you go to the right, that happens. If you choose this partner, something else happens. It's not set in stone. It's variable. The program is giving you all these options, and that's how life is.

We want to figure out, hey, what's a cool future path? Instead of worrying about the details, of what actions you have to do to get there, you're just going to set some suggestions, look at the big picture, visit it, and say, "Oh, that's really cool," and then maybe see some details. Then your subconscious and your gut are going to be programmed for that happy future, and you're just going to naturally start doing it.

You're going to naturally wake up in the morning and just start noticing that pull. It'll be like a magnetic pull. Maybe you'll do something different. Maybe you'll put your left shoe on instead of your right shoe on first, if you did it vice versa. Maybe you'll stop putting creamer in your coffee whereas you used to put a bunch in before. There's no right or wrong. It's just noticing the difference. Start noticing, hmm, I'm feeling pulled to do something out of my ordinary pattern, out of my persona. That's a good thing. You want to mix it up. That will help you to create what you want.

The script is going to help you visit whatever near future your subconscious feels you need to look at. There are infinite possibilities, so we could be here forever—which, you know, would be kind of fun.

You can create whatever place you'd like in your consciousness—you can create a wonderful place to go to. You can. So why not start creating it now. Right? Let's get in the mode of "I deserve wonderful things." Think big! Like, not just a nice person to talk to. That's good. We're all nice. Big! Like a loving, blissful place—a wonderful opportunity for everyone. Start thinking big. Open up. You have nothing to lose. It's all there to create...

In your subconscious, there really isn't past, present, future, so it doesn't really matter how linear you are, but just to make it easier on your mind, we're going to visit possible futures for your life—a really great, fun, big, exciting future—and help you create that. You can have amazing things. I hear it all the time. That's what I want for you—whether it's a wonderful mate, house, job, being at the beach every day. Just being happy at your core. At the core, stuff doesn't really matter. I don't have anything against stuff. But happiness comes from within, and then the pretty stuff makes you even more fun and happy. If you don't have it inside, no matter if you think of and get a red Maserati tomorrow, it wouldn't make a difference, right?

Since you have infinite future possibilities, you will want some conscious clarity about where you want to visit in your future. I invite you to get clear about what's important to you. I suggest you review your life vision statement (from Chapter 1) before reading the following meditation.

This exercise is called the New You meditation exercise. This exercise is one way to induce alpha state or a meditative state. You will need at least 30–40 minutes without interruptions to practice this particular exercise.

NOTE: You may find it helpful to slowly read the following script a few times to get used to it, and then read it into an audio recorder to play back for yourself as you stay in a relaxed position. However, you can still learn to reach a relaxed meditative state if you choose to participate with your eyes open (or closed) without recording the script.

To Begin

Now, take a deep breath. Place your hands on the belly. It's always good to get centered in your core... You can go wherever you like; you're always safe, and you're the master of your destiny. So, get comfortable... Close your eyes.

And just begin to notice your breath, and in this journey, you're the master of your destiny and master of your journey. So all you need to do is follow along with these directions... You don't need to do anything at all... There's no effort required; it's just being.

If you'd like to lie down, that's fine too, but it's nice to learn this process in a seated posture, so you can do it any time, any place... And to go more deeply within, letting your conscious mind know it's safe... And if you'd like to picture your conscious mind as an observer that helps to watch out for you during the day, you can have it as a guard, like a guard dog or a cat, to give it a persona. And just ask it for the next little while to wait out-side... It's still a part of you, but it doesn't have to worry, or be concerned... So you can picture it as your guard critter that waits outside; maybe it sits on a nice tree branch.

Or lays down on the soft grass out front, and it's still there observing you and protecting you, but not as vigilant because you're safe in here. And if you'd like to search in your mind's eye, in your consciousness for a guide, for a wise guide who will help you on your journey, you can ask your subconscious mind to show you that person or symbol now... And just have a feeling or a sense of that person with you... If you don't see details of that wise guide, that's fine; you may just get an emotional, kinesthetic sense of a wise person helping you, guiding you... It may even be your representation of your higher self.

Take in a few deep breaths into the belly and notice this wise guide. And any sounds you hear outside, around you, in your room ... wherever you're at, just imagine that they help you relax even more... That you're safe... If ever you hear any rustling, or people chatting, or cars going by, those help your subconscious mind to go even more deeply within.

Breathing in through the nose ... filling up with oxygen ... all the way into the deep part of the belly, and exhaling, releasing any concerns of the day. And imagine in your mind's eye that you're in a restful place... Maybe your favorite place in nature, wherever that is... Imagine in this place that you're sitting on a large comfortable tree stump that's just right for your height... Just your size to sit on comfortably to sit on for a few moments. Imagining the tree roots growing down into the center of the earth. Many of you may be familiar with this as a good grounding exercise from a previous script in the book... Imagine those tree roots going all the way down past the rocks and dirt, past the layers of earth, into the earth's magnetic core, and exhaling out any concerns into that tree root, into the earth's center.

And as you breathe in, imagine over your head is the warm golden sun warming you, filling you up with fresh chi, with fresh energy from the day... And exhaling, releasing down into the earth... Releasing any fears or concerns, releasing any external distractions.

Begin to imagine even releasing any old patterns that hold you back ... known or unknown... Any old patterns from childhood or from old memories ... any past that you may feel may hold you back from creating what you want... And you may not even have a conscious awareness of what these are...

That's fine... Just allow your subconscious to have its own awareness.

And begin to scan your body from the top of your head all the way down to the tips of your toes, releasing any old patterns stored in your body. We tend to store patterns in our body, that's what we create... So as you do your scan from the top of your head all the way down into your abdomen and into your legs, down through your feet and toes, imagine your subconscious mind finding any last little residual bits of old patterns... Anything about struggle or discomfort—known or unknown.

Imagine you can release those with the breath, exhaling, releasing out... Making space for new patterns and to activate dormant patterns of happiness... And as you're feeling relaxed and feeling safer, imagine in front of you, a beautiful staircase of your own design ... a beautiful railing ... and whatever else you'd like to add to that staircase... It has ten steps going down into a beautiful safe garden.

Begin to allow yourself to go down into those steps, down the ten steps... At the bottom is a beautiful safe garden... Gently go down the ninth step... The eighth step... Down the seventh ... with each step, going more deeply into a state of peace and openness... Starting to open to possibilities of your future life... Down the sixth step... Almost there, down past the fifth... Going down those last few steps at your own pace ... counting down the fourth step to the bottom step ... and whenever you reach that bottom step, and your foot touches down to the ground in the safe garden, you feel even more at peace and calm and ready to begin your journey into a happy future.

And you'll start this by noticing three doorways at the base of the safe garden... Notice three doorways in front of you... And the left doorway has a white tint to it with a gold handle... The middle doorway has a red tint; you can choose the handle color... And the third doorway has a blue tint, and here you can also choose the handle color. Just notice what comes to you... And if you're more auditory or kinesthetic, you may notice a tone associated with the doorway or feel the texture of the door... However it comes to you is just fine.

Just begin to let that sensation come to you in whatever way feels comfortable... Feeling safe and warm and at ease... At peace... Knowing at your core the sense of peace, and love, and fulfillment... No matter what happens on your external daily journey, you know you can activate and be in touch with this sense of peace and happiness... It's there no matter what's going on around you in the illusion of daily life.

In a moment, you're going to pick one of those three doorways to visit... And behind the doorway, allow your subconscious mind to start to choose, out of your vast storehouse of future life possibilities, choose one future possibility to visit behind one of those doors that's for your highest happiness, health, prosperity, relationship happiness, and life satisfaction. Whatever you would like to experience on this journey called life ... allowing that to happen behind one of those doors.

It can be a near future time or next year... It doesn't matter... Whatever your subconscious would like to experience to help you align with this present life to be happier and to help you create this future life... And every step you take ... every action you take ... creating this future life.

So let those details start to form more clearly, whether sounds, or words, or pictures, or colors, or feelings ... they start to form behind that doorway... And one of the three doors gets very bright, and you feel pulled towards it... Now count from one to three, and when you get to three, that doorway will gently come open, and you'll walk into that life.

One, letting those details clearly form even more ... two, more and more details forming for your health, happiness, and welfare ... and three, letting that doorway gently swing open...

And let yourself be drawn to that door and over the threshold, floating, walking, sauntering, however, you'd like to go through that doorway... Almost like there's a magnetism that draws you in, that you're safe to experience the details

And as you go across the threshold, let that door close gently behind you... Hearing the door close... All the background sounds you've heard helping your subconscious mind to feel that, so that you can more fully experience that future now... And just rest there quietly for a few minutes ... finding a place to sit or lie down, gently breathing into the belly and letting the details start to come to you... They may come quickly or slowly ... just take a moment to notice the first detail. Whatever you notice or don't notice is just right for you...

Breathing in through the belly, resting in this place, maybe a new day is dawning here. Notice if there are any birds overhead... Notice who's around you... Notice your emotional state in this place... Notice in this new place, this new future, notice the feelings in your belly... Just check in... Ask your subconscious how you feel... Breathing that in... And if you're watching it like a movie, it may be more movie-like... You may be watching a future you distantly like a movie... So take that in... You may feel it or watch it more visually as pictures on a screen... So, if that's the case for you, ask yourself in that movie, your movie self, how are you feeling?

Instead of a feeling in your gut, you may get a word from that future self. Take a moment to be with that quietly... Breathing that in... Noticing your future self... Watching yourself like a movie... And in your future, there are many possibilities. Notice where you are... Maybe a different place than you're used to being... Allow your mind to open up to the possibilities... Ask yourself, where am I? And take a moment quietly to notice... And if you're new to meditating or focusing, be gentle with yourself... You don't need to be in deep trance to get information... Just notice as you breathe in … dropping more fully into that state of being … that place … the future of happiness and joy and wonderful peace. As you exhale, exhale out any blocks to being in that place.

Imagine hearing them drop out like blocks, down those roots you've created earlier, so they may plunk … plunk … drop out of the roots like little rocks. And any sounds you hear around you help to draw out those rocks and add to that symphony of plunk … allowing any blocks in the present day to release.

Imagine breathing in from the top of your head down into the belly and into the legs, scanning and noticing … Imagining the gold from the sun above you being like a wash, to help you wash out any blocks to being there, to being in this wonderful happy future… Floating in that peacefulness… Let yourself float in that love … that bliss. And if you need to ask yourself again in this future movie, ask where you are? Then, listen quietly.

Take in whatever information you need to take in… And look around you now, in your future … and notice who you're with … maybe people you know from the present, and maybe new people, and maybe people from long ago. Just look around for a moment quietly and notice… Saying hello… Greeting… Whatever you need to do in that place, you'll feel magnetically drawn to do. Take a moment or two to notice any other things you feel drawn to do there… Breathing in that information… Breathing in support and acceptance.

Noticing that acceptance of your needs … your desires … any old misbeliefs of discomfort or needing to suffer get washed away. Imagine them washed away with your breath … with the air floating by you… Imagining all that releasing as you exhale… Imagine it floating away like a cloud, anything you need to let go of… Saying goodbye to it. Watching it float off into the distant horizon… Breathing in the sense of new possibilities.

And for one more minute, walking around this place, taking in the colors, the sounds, the smells, the people, the feelings, the sensations ... whatever you need to take in. You'll remember whatever you need to remember... It may come up to you in dreams or insights over the next few days or weeks... For now, just let those float into your awareness; and later, if you'd like, you can write down what you notice at the end... For now, let it wash over you, feeling this place, whether as a movie or all senses and every cell of your body... You choose... Breathing in that sensation... Noticing whatever information you need to know.

In a moment, you're going to say goodbye to this place in the future, knowing it's yours to create whenever you'd like, whether distant or sooner. You're going to leave this place now and step over the threshold of that door, and come back into the present, that safe garden ... and stay relaxed to do a different journey in a minute. For now, say goodbye to that future... Goodbye to those people, knowing they're always there with you... Everything exists right here, right now... As we have infinite futures available to us at all times to choose from.

With this one though, imagine the door closing, as it goes into your file system of your subconscious mind... Imagine as you exhale all the parts of you—body, mind, and awareness—line up for your own highest good and happiness.... Only you know what that is... You can choose your own highest happiness... And resting for a few moments in this safe garden.

Imagine, whenever you're ready, a beautiful movie screen with red velvet curtains appears in front of your mind's eye. And those red curtains begin to pull back on the count of three... And behind those beautiful velvet red and gold curtains is a portion of a possible future in your life... Letting yourself gently go to whatever part of your future you need to see for this space of time... Your subconscious mind knows where to go to take you to that place you've already thought of when you reviewed your goals internally for where you want to be in this life... About how to pattern in your life and instill helpful change—just like the app metaphor we discussed throughout the book.

This exercise is called Pattern Change meditation exercise. This exercise is one way to induce alpha state or a meditative state. You will need at least 15–20 minutes without interruptions to practice this particular exercise.

NOTE: You may find it helpful to slowly read the following script a few times to get used to it, and then read it into an audio recorder to play back for yourself as you stay in a relaxed position. However, you can still learn to reach a relaxed meditative state if you choose to participate with your eyes open (or closed) without recording the script.

To Begin

Get comfortable, close your eyes, and start to notice your breath... Dropping into your body. One key skill to know is that of grounding your body.

One way you can do this is to notice the base of your spine, and imagine that you're out in nature. Somewhere comfortable and cozy ... your favorite place... And you're sitting on a large, comfortable tree stump that's just right for your height... And the tree roots grow down into the center of the earth... And begin to imagine you're one with the tree, almost as if the roots are part of you, from the base of your spine... And imagine the roots go all the way down past the rocks, past the dirt, past the shale, all the layers of the earth, and they drop into the center of the earth, where the earth's magma is, the magnetic core. This represents a place to recycle and release any thing that may be weighing you down. The magnetic magma is a place to melt away stress and tension...

And begin to get a body sense of what that would be like... Magma spinning around... The magnetic flow of the earth on those roots. Drop into that, and know this is a safe place to be... Imagine being completely safe and comfortable, watching those roots go down into the center of the earth... Watching from

activate a sense of happiness and peace and have fulfilling work and relationships... Your subconscious mind knows where to take you in this future. This future is another option for you.

So as you count from one to three, notice those beautiful velvet curtains slowly opening and beginning to take you there to this future place ... one, opening a little more ... two, even more ... and three, they're fully pulled back ... and on the screen that movie of your future begins to gently, quietly play in front of you... And ask your subconscious if you'd like to step into the movie and be part of it, like a 4-D experience... Breathing in all the details of the movie... Or if you'd like to sit back on a comfy, plush seat in the movie theater, while watching that movie of your future... You can do that... You can choose... Allowing your subconscious mind to choose that... Notice where you go, floating off into that future... Knowing you're in charge of creating that future... A happy, peaceful, beautiful future... Be there now.

And notice the colors... What's the first color you see? As you feel the weight of your hands on your lap or wherever they're resting, you go to that future place now, even more easily... Feeling the weight of gravity tug gently on your body, breathing that in... Being there for a few moments, a short visit this time... Seeing which people you're with... Maybe you notice what you're doing, what you're saying, what you're wearing... Breathing that in... Who you're talking to... And notice in your belly how you're feeling. Again, if you're new to this, and watching yourself as a movie, ask your movie self, how you're feeling... Take a moment quietly to notice.

And if you'd like to create a relationship as part of your future, see yourself having it now. Notice whom you're with... Take a moment to notice that person or people, whether friendships or romantic ... just notice who's in your life and is important to you... Notice who's welcoming you... Notice your community... Feeling a sense of spaciousness, yet connectedness to your community... These are the people who support you in your life... And in this future place, you're with community of supportive, loving people.

If you'd like to create a wonderful job, or business, or philanthropic endeavor in your future, notice a few details of what got you there... Take a moment to notice that now... Feeling a sense of accomplishment... Thanking yourself for getting yourself there... And giving your subconscious body, mind, and spirit the suggestion, the program, the positive program to instill in you a magnet... A loving, happy magnet that will pull you naturally to where you want to be, to that loving relationship, programming the magnet for that.

All the possibilities of loving people in your life ... that can be programming the magnet for that... For your loving supportive family and community ... programming the magnet for that... Breathing that in ... feeling the heaviness of that ... in that future place... For that enjoyable work, vacation, philanthropic endeavor ... whatever you'd like to fill your time with ... whether it's traditional work or something else, that's just fine... Filling your time with enjoyable pursuits, noticing that now... And programming the magnet for that... So that magnet is going to draw you easily to the action steps you need to take for that loving happy future.

And if you need a moment to program the magnet for anything else, maybe optimal health, do that now... Breathing that in, letting it activate in the belly and all cells of your being... Seeing that future self, saying hello, seeing happiness on that future self's face, and in all cells of its being... And letting that resonate with you now... Ask your wise guide that you connected with in the beginning to help you with that... It may be felt quietly on the sidelines or more obviously... Either way is fine... Feeling a sense of supportiveness resonate in your being... And taking a moment, a last moment to look around in this future place... Notice any

details you may need to notice... They may come across as a color, a phrase ... whatever it is, just notice.

And let it quietly percolate in all cells of your being, body, mind, and spirit. Again it may mature over days or weeks; you may see more of it in dreams... But know this place is there for you at any time you'd like to go there... It's there in the back of your mind... For now though, begin to say goodbye to that future self, thanking her for all her help... Feeling a sense of gratitude and pleasure for the journey... And breathing into the belly.

At your own pace, begin to quietly leave that movie screen, that place... Letting those curtains close... Clearing out the space there. Leaving those three doors also ... and the peaceful garden... Begin to walk up, gradually up the ten steps... From the tenth bottom step up to the top first step at your own pace... So going from the tenth to the ninth, up to the eight and so on... Gently, slowly ... with each step up ... bringing a little more of your awareness into the body, into your present time.

With each breath in, feeling more fully present, bringing all parts of yourself back in from the future. And when you reach that top first step, you can gradually, slowly open your eyes... And maybe pat your body, pat your knees, rub your hands together; maybe wiggle your feet and toes... And then take a few minutes to stretch and do whatever you need to do to return to your room feeling refreshed and invigorated.

A BASIC PATTERN CHANGE MEDITATION

This is a new meditation. This script will teach you how to get into a basic relaxed alpha meditation state to help you change an unhelpful

above, from where you're sitting, and as you exhale anything you need to release anything you need to let go of and let it drop down those tree roots... So as you breathe in, and you exhale out, let the tree roots grow a little more... With each exhale, releasing a little more of whatever you need to release.

And let's imagine that your conscious mind can be like a cat, and it can sit out on one of the trees outside the room ... and just watch you and let the conscious mind rest for a little bit. Imagine the subconscious mind is percolating up, and let's just set the intention for whatever's in your highest good ... the ultimate goal being happiness and balance ... that your conscious and subconscious minds align with that highest goal of happiness and balance. Whatever that looks like for you ... you have a unique signature and way of being... And what feels like happiness to one person is different for the next.

And let's imagine the logical conscious mind can just rest like that cat taking a cat nap on a branch out front... Imagine any worries, any concerns, any fears can be washed away with your breath ... you'll feel safe, calm, and protected as you notice your breath...

Breathing in to the belly, exhaling, releasing any residual tensions down that tree root... And let's begin to gently scan the body from the top of your head, all the way down to the tips of your toes... And imagine as you scan the body, you have a bright yellow sun above your head, and that it can scan through your body from the top of your head all the way down to the tops of your toes... And you can breathe in that gold color as you scan your body; it goes through the face and the cheeks and the jaw, into the throat, filling up the chest... And this gold color symbolizes unconditional love for you and others, and also symbolizes healing in your life patterns. Gold is a healing color.

So let that gold color rest in the chest, cleansing out the heart, down into the ribs, and if you feel your conscious mind drifting off, that's fine. Your subconscious mind still gets the message, still gets the healing... Breathing into the belly, down through the arms, letting that gold wash through all the cells and the organs of the belly... Cleansing out any old patterns that no longer serve you... Whether it's a relationship pattern, a love pattern, a health pattern, a money pattern. Let's set the intention that the gold color, that gold sun, as it washes through the body, clears out any of those old patterns.

And imagine you can open up the cells to release that old pattern, letting that gold color wash through the legs, down through the calves, out the feet, out the soles of the feet... Good. Breathing it in, opening up every cell of the body into that gold color. And imagining the cells opening and releasing down those roots... Breathing in, opening up the belly especially, and just noticing what's there... Noticing where you hold any old tensions, especially behind the belly button and around that area... Imagine you can breathe in fresh new energy, breathing that in behind the belly... Washing over the top of the head and down through the soles of the feet.

And as you do so, you feel an electrical surge of happiness and a sense of calm and peace at your center, opening up to that possibility... And if that possibility is new to you, imagine you're watching it from a distance on a movie screen. And if you'd like, you can be a part of that movie screen, experiencing it in all dimensions and all senses, watching what it's like to be completely calm and at ease, connected with a sense of universal love for yourself, for others... And notice what that would look like... What's one thing you would be saying to a friend, a neighbor, or an acquaintance if you felt that sense of universal love? When you feel that, what do you think you would be saying? Imagine hearing that now... Where would you feel that in your body? And even if you're in a light trance or a deep trance—either way the subconscious gets the message... Letting that sense of peacefulness and happiness, activate maybe even 75 percent more throughout the body.

A Basic Pattern Change Meditation

Allow yourself to have that for a moment... Or for however long you would like. Breathing that into the belly, feeling the breath, bring that into the belly... And ask your subconscious mind to show you one place you hold on to an old pattern that no longer serves you, whether it's on relationships, health, work or prosperity. Just notice one place in the body where you hold that pattern. First place that pops up. Imagine putting a color to that old pattern that you would like to release... Usually a murky pattern color for that pattern. And put that murky color there, feeling that pattern... Imagine it's a shape... Ask your subconscious mind to show you what shape that pattern is. For example, if in the distant past, you dated people you felt weren't a good match, what shape is that pattern? It may pop up as a triangle, a square, or a circle... Any shape is fine... Just notice, and put a shape to that pattern... This is the unhelpful pattern that you'd like to release.

Take a moment to check in and imagine finding that pattern, a shape and a color... Breathing into that. Imagine as you breathe in, the cells can open up, and they can begin to release that pattern... And let's put a place, a receptacle for it out in the storage locker of the "all possible." Imagine 30 feet in front of you to the right is a big storage container where all the old patterns you'd like to release can go... Imagine those murky triangles, squares, circles, or whatever they are, start floating out with the breath... Old parts of you that you'd like to release... You can talk to those parts of you if you'd like.

You're made up of many parts... Many parts to your personality, your persona. And you change them all the time. Many puzzle pieces make up your whole. So, you can acknowledge the puzzle piece and say that this one no longer fits there... Exhale out that shape, that color, and let it go into that holding space way out in front of you to the right... With each breath, releasing more, letting the cells open up, releasing... And imagine you do that body scan from the top of your head all the way down

*through your cheeks and jaw, into your throat, down into the
chest, into the belly, opening up. Take a moment to quietly scan
your own body. Imagining where that pattern may need to be
released from... And release it now.*

*And if you need to go into deep trance to release this, that's
fine. You may even feel it's almost like sleep for a few moments...
That's fine... Just let it release... Imagining those old blocks to
relationship, money, work, and feeling motivation and clarity...
Releasing whatever you need to release now, feeling it release, saying goodbye to it... And as you exhale on the breath, it quietly
goes of its own accord... Just watch that process for a moment
quietly... Watching the pattern exude like a cloud, floating off
into that holding space. Breathing in deeply, exhaling deeply.*

*And then when you feel like you're sufficiently emptied out,
anywhere you've released from, imagine you can breathe in that
bright golden sun as a representation of a neutral you... Breathing that in, into the present, filling up with that sun in all the
spaces you've released from... And then imagine in your mind's
eye that your new pattern related to your goal is out there in the
"all possible"... And give that new goal, that new pattern a
shape... Ask your subconscious mind to show you... Whatever it
is, any shape is fine... Just notice the first thing that pops into your
awareness. And imagine you're at the "all possible" store of possibilities, and you can go and pick that shape, and this represents
your happy relationships, your happy workspace, your happy
health situation, prosperity, and your goals... You may feel an
ah-hah, or a lock, like this is it... Give yourself a few moments
to search for that.*

*You may even want to picture the new goal in the shape of a
flower, or some symbol that's meaningful to you... And if you'd
like help, imagine a wise guide coming to you and helping you
pick a pattern of your highest happiness, health, and well-being...
And imagine that source of help assisting you... It may be your*

own inner knowing, your own higher self. However you'd like to conceptualize it, that's fine.

And you may begin feeling in the belly a kind of movement, a magnetic change, a shift, an awareness as that new pattern drops into the belly, the source of the subconscious. You may want to use your breath to help you lock that in place, almost like you're downloading a new computer program or app... You've released the old one and you've brought in a new one... And imagine in the next week, and the next 30 days, you allow yourself to fully download this new program or app... And you notice changes—maybe subtle, maybe large, but you notice them... Breathing in those awarenesses, maybe even seeing yourself a few days out into the future, a few weeks out into the future, having what you wanted... It's already happened... It's already there... Breathing in that color, breathing in that shape... Exhaling down those roots, any auditory, verbal arguments against you having what you want... Imagine those little mind chatters just float by as you exhale... They float away; no big deal.

And then begin to slowly bring your awareness back into the room with the next three breaths, breathing in, three up to one. At your own pace, and in your own way, begin to bring your awareness more fully into your body, and into the present moment. Seeing yourself having that state of being already... Happiness and well-being, already there, completely calm and at ease... And as you bring yourself back into the room, with that final count up, you feel relaxed yet alert, ready to move on with the rest of your day.

Begin to wiggle your feet and your toes, your hands. Maybe rub your palms together, stretch your legs, and then take a few moments of quiet to reconnect with your body... And after that, take a few moments to process what you experienced in whatever way you would like.

REVIEW—
BODY SCAN MEDITATION EXERCISE

NOTE: You may find it helpful to slowly read the following script a few times to get used to it, and then read it into an audio recorder to play back for yourself as you stay in a relaxed position. However, you can still learn to reach a relaxed meditative state if you choose to participate with your eyes open (or closed) without recording the script.

This exercise is called the Body Scan meditation exercise and is one way to induce alpha state or a meditative state. You will need at least 10–15 minutes without interruptions to practice this exercise.

To Begin

Get as comfortable as you can in your chair with both feet flat on the ground. Take a moment now to close your eyes and make sure you are comfortable.

Now, begin to mentally scan your body: start with the very top of your head, through your forehead and neck, progressing slowly all the way down through each part of your body at your own pace, visiting each part of the body, even down to the soles of your feet. As you bring awareness down into every area of your body, notice any place that you may hold stress or tension (pause)... Just notice them for now, recognize these spots, and then move on, continuing to slowly scan your whole body, becoming curious about what your body feels like (pause)...

Allow yourself to take some relaxed, open belly breaths, letting the air fill your lungs and press into the belly ... feeling the rise and fall of your belly (pause)... Now imagine that your breath goes to one of the tight or tense areas... Notice as the breath goes there ... the area begins to loosen and relax. Loosening ... relaxing... Again, breathe gently into that area ... feeling relaxed ... breathing gently ... loosening ... and relaxing ...

loosening and relaxing even more... You may choose to bring the breath to another part of the body and that new area begins to loosen and relax (pause)...

Take a moment to notice the thoughts in your head. Just notice what's there right now ... you don't have to do anything with them or to them... Notice... What are you thinking right now?... Do you see the thoughts float in front of your mind's eye?... Where do you sense the thoughts?... Where do they reside in your body?... Breathe gently and just be curious (pause)...

Let the thoughts turn into clouds ... floating... In the blue sky... Of your mind's eye. Allow the thoughts to just float by you... Each thought turning into a white, fluffy cloud... Watch them float by you for a moment... Notice each thought in your mind transform easily... And let it float by (pause)... Observe and... Let them go with each breath... Notice you may feel like a neutral observer... Watching... Unattached... Watching the clouds disappear into the horizon... Smaller... With each moment... The blue sky becomes clearer and clearer... The clouds floating away... Disappearing... Breathing gently (pause)...

Imagine that the blue sky becomes you... Becomes your whole body... Notice your whole body... From your head down to your toes... As you inhale... Allowing this calming, radiant blue sky to fill your whole body and mind for a moment, completely clear... Completely calm... Completely at ease in the clarity... Enlarge the blue sky just a bit and let it fill you even more... Relaxing into your breath...

Notice that the calmness and clarity helps you... Helps you to naturally access any tools... Any information you need now in your daily life... As you take another gentle breath, notice you are more calm, more relaxed, more at ease (pause)...

When you are ready, open your eyes, bring yourself back into the room, stretch and notice that you feel more relaxed, yet recharged. In this way, you may move into the next phase of your day.

REVIEW—
SAFE PLACE GUIDED MEDITATION

This is the Safe Place Guided Meditation. This exercise is one way to induce alpha state or a meditative state. You will need at least 10–15 minutes without interruptions to practice this exercise.

NOTE: You may find it helpful to slowly read the following script a few times to get used to it, and then read it into an audio recorder to play back for yourself as you stay in a relaxed position. However, you can still learn to reach a relaxed meditative state if you choose to participate with your eyes open (or closed) without recording the script.

To begin this guided meditation, I invite you to sit or lie down in a comfortable position and close your eyes. Kindly notice your body and be aware of any tension. As you exhale, notice the tension leaving your body as your breath flows out. Allow your breathing to gradually slow down at your own pace... Just tuning into the breath for however long feels good to you...

As you do this, allow yourself to picture in your mind a safe place. Notice what the first comes to mind. What type of place does your mind choose as a safe place...?

Some people choose a natural setting, like a beach or meadow. If it's a beach, what do the waves look like? What do they sound like? Some people may feel the mist on their face? Taste the salt on your tongue... Allow yourself to notice if there any birds overhead. You may hear the sound of the birds chirping, singing a song. Notice if there are any breezes in this place, feel the wind on your cheeks...

Notice the ground beneath your feet. Is it dirt or sand, or maybe something else? What does it feel like on your feet? Just know that whatever you experience here is just right for you…

Allow yourself to lie down in the safe place and feel the ground beneath your body. Notice the gentle ground below warming your body, allowing you to relax even more and feel safe and comfortable during this meditation. Feel the weight of your body resting on the ground allowing gravity to help you release any tension into the ground and let go of it. Imagine that with each breath you breathe that any tension gets washed away with the breath… Look above you into this sky and notice the color of the sky. Is the sun shining? Is the sky clear? Notice if there any trees around. What kind of leaves do they have? What color are the leaves? Pick one of the leaves and notice what it feels like, what's the texture like?

Then, notice a tree stump in this place. If you feel like it, go and sit on this stump, feeling the sun above your head warming you and further relaxing you. Breathe in the warmth and vibrancy of the sun, allowing it to fill you with a sense of calm and peace from the top of your head to the tips of your toes. As you become part of your safe place, notice that you feel more rested, more relaxed, more at peace… When you're ready, allow yourself to come back into this room and leave your safe place for now, knowing that at any time you can return to your safe place, anytime you need… After you have thoroughly connected with this place, open your eyes. In the same relaxed position, continue to breathe smoothly and rhythmically, and take a few moments to experience and enjoy your relaxing guided meditation. Your safe place is available to you whenever you need to go there.

PROGRESSIVE MUSCLE RELAXATION— A GUIDED MEDITATION

If you would like another new way of reaching a meditative state, here is another option. Progressive muscle relaxation is a good technique for getting into a relaxed alpha state. In the 1930s, Dr. Edmund Jacobson discovered that tensing and releasing various muscle groups throughout the body produces a state of relaxation.

In his original book, *Progressive Relaxation*, Dr. Jacobson developed a series of hundreds of different muscle relaxation exercises and an elaborate training program. More recently, the system has been abbreviated to a few basic exercises, which are just as effective if practiced regularly. The following script is one I developed for my clients, incorporating my own tools and unique wording.

This exercise is called Progressive Muscle Relaxation exercise. This exercise is one way to induce alpha state or a meditative state. You will need at least 15–20 minutes without interruptions to practice this particular exercise.

NOTE: You may find it helpful to slowly read the following script a few times to get used to it, and then read it into an audio recorder to play back for yourself as you stay in a relaxed position. However, you can still learn to reach a relaxed meditative state if you choose to participate with your eyes open (or closed) without recording the script.

To Begin

Start by getting into a comfortable position. Close your eyes. Place the feet flat on the floor, legs uncrossed and your hands resting comfortably at your side or on your lap. Begin by noticing your breathing, noticing your abdomen rise and fall with each breath. As your breathing becomes more relaxed and restful, take your awareness down to your feet. We will start this process with the muscles in the feet and toes. When I say "tense" you will tense the muscles in the feet by curling the toes down and holding for a count of four full seconds and then will release the muscles in the feet when I say "release," and will repeat this process two times in various muscle groups throughout the body. Ready... So, with your awareness in the feet and toes now tense the feet and hold for one ... two ... three ... four..., and "release."

Notice the difference between a tense muscle and a relaxed muscle as you go through the process. Remembering to inhale through the nose and exhale through the mouth, releasing any residual tension in the feet. With each tense and release cycle, you will notice it becomes easier and easier to release and relax each muscle group... Now again, bring your awareness to the feet and toes and "tense" and hold for one ... two ... three ... four..., and release ... inhaling through the nose and exhaling through the mouth, relaxing even more with each breath. Now, we will move our awareness to the lower legs ... to the calf area. When I say "tense," we will tense these muscles by pointing the toes towards the knees, and again holding for a count of three, and then releasing the calf muscles. Ready... So, with your awareness in the calf muscles now tense the calves and hold for one ... two ... three ... four..., and "release." Notice the difference between a tense muscle and a relaxed muscle as you go through the process. Remembering to inhale through the nose and exhale through the mouth, releasing any residual tension in the calves.

With each tense and release cycle, you will notice it becomes easier and easier to release and relax each muscle group... Now again, bring your awareness to the calves and "tense" and hold for one ... two ... three ... four..., and release ... inhaling through the nose and exhaling through the mouth, relaxing even more with each breath. Notice the muscles in the thighs. When I say "tense," we will tense the muscles in the thighs by pressing the back of the legs in the bottom of the chair and holding for a count of four seconds and then release. Ready... So, with your awareness in the thighs now tense and hold for one ... two ... three ... four..., and "release." Notice the difference between a tense muscle and a relaxed muscle as you go through the process. Remembering to inhale through the nose and exhale through the mouth, releasing any residual tension in the thighs.

With each cycle, you notice it becomes easier and easier to release and relax each muscle group... Now again, bring your awareness to the thighs and "tense" and hold for one ... two ... three ... four..., and release ... inhaling through the nose and exhaling through the mouth, relaxing even more with each breath. Now, notice the muscles in the abdomen and low back. When I say "tense," we will tense the muscles in the abdomen by imagining that we are trying to touch the belly button to the spine, pressing the low back to the chair and holding for a count of four seconds and then release. Ready... So, with your awareness in the abdomen, now tense and hold for one ... two ... three ... four..., and "release." Notice the difference between a tense muscle and a relaxed muscle again. Remembering to inhale through the nose and exhale through the mouth, releasing any residual tension in the low back and abdomen.

With each cycle, you notice it becomes easier and easier to release and relax each muscle group... Now again, bring your awareness to the abdomen, "tense" and hold for one ... two ... three ... four..., and release ... inhaling through the nose and exhaling through the mouth, relaxing even more with each breath. Bring your awareness to the muscles in the right arm. When I say "tense," we will tense the muscles in the right arm by curling the arm up towards your bicep and holding it as if you are lifting a weight and holding it to your chest, holding for a count of four seconds and then release. Ready... So, with your awareness in the arm now tense and hold for one ... two ... three ... four..., and "release." Notice the difference between a tense muscle and a relaxed muscle as you go through the process again. Remembering to inhale through the nose and exhale through the mouth, releasing any residual tension in the arm. With each cycle, you notice it becomes easier and easier to release and relax each muscle group... Now again, bring your awareness to the arm and "tense" and hold for one ... two ... three ... four..., and release ... inhaling through the nose and exhaling through the mouth, relaxing even more with each breath.

Now, bring your awareness to the muscles in the right hand. When I say "tense," we will tense the muscles in the right hand by clenching it into a tight fist, holding for a count of four seconds and then release. Ready... So, with your awareness in the hand, now tense and hold for one ... two ... three ... four..., and "release." Notice the difference between a tense muscle and a relaxed muscle as you go through the process again. Remembering to inhale through the nose and exhale through the mouth, releasing any residual tension in the arm. With each cycle, you notice it becomes easier and easier to release and relax each muscle group... Now again, bring your awareness to the hand and "tense" and hold for one ... two ... three ... four..., and release ... inhaling through the nose and exhaling through the mouth, relaxing even more with each breath. Bring your awareness to the muscles in the left arm. When I say "tense," we will tense the muscles in the left arm by curling the arm up towards your bicep and holding it as if you are lifting a weight and holding it to your chest, holding for a count of four seconds and then release.

Ready... So, with your awareness in the arm now tense and hold for one ... two ... three ... four..., and "release." Notice the difference between a tense muscle and a relaxed muscle as you go through the process again. Remembering to inhale through the nose and exhale through the mouth, releasing any residual tension in the arm. With each cycle, you notice it becomes easier and easier to release and relax each muscle group... Now, bring your awareness to the arm and "tense" and hold for one ... two ... three ... four..., and release ... inhaling through the nose and exhaling through the mouth, relaxing even more with each breath. Now, bring your awareness to the muscles in the left hand. When I say "tense," we will tense the muscles in the left hand by clenching it *into a tight fist, holding for a count of four seconds and then release. Ready... So, with your awareness in the left hand, now tense and hold for one ... two ... three ... four..., and "release." Notice the difference between a tense muscle and a relaxed one. Remembering to inhale through the nose and exhale through the mouth, releasing any residual tension in the arm. With each cycle, you notice it becomes easier and easier to release and relax each muscle group ... again, bring your awareness to the hand and "tense" and hold for one ... two ... three ... four..., and release ... inhaling through the nose and exhaling through the mouth, relaxing even more with each breath.*

Notice the muscles in the upper back, around the shoulder blades. When I say "tense," we will tense the muscles in the upper back by pressing the shoulder blades together and holding for a count of four seconds and then release. Ready... So, with your awareness in the shoulder blades, now tense and hold for one ... two ... three ... four..., and "release." Notice the difference between tense and relaxed as you go through the process. Remembering to inhale through the nose and exhale through the mouth, releasing any residual tension. With each cycle, you notice it becomes easier and easier to release and relax each muscle group... Now again, bring your awareness to the upper back and "tense" and hold for one ... two ... three ... four, and release ... inhaling through the nose and exhaling through the mouth, relaxing even more with each breath. Notice the muscles in the shoulder area and neck. When I say "tense" we will tense the muscles in the neck by pressing the shoulders towards the ears and holding for a count of four seconds and then release. Ready... So, with your awareness in the neck and shoulders, now tense and hold for one ... two ... three ... four..., and "release." Notice the difference between a tense muscle and a relaxed muscle as you go through the process.

Remembering to inhale through the nose and exhale through the mouth, releasing any residual tension in this area ... it becomes easier and easier to release and relax each muscle group... Now again, bring your awareness to the shoulders and "tense" and hold for one ... two ... three ... four..., and release ... inhaling through the nose and exhaling through the mouth, relaxing even more with each breath. Bring your awareness to the chin and jaw area. When I say "tense" we will tense the muscles in the jaw by pressing the chin into the chest, gently and holding for a count of four seconds and then release. Ready... So, with your awareness in the chin and around the jaw area, now tense and hold for one ... two... three ... four..., and "release." Again, noticing the difference between a tense muscle and a relaxed muscle as you go through the process. Remembering to inhale through the nose and exhale through the mouth, releasing any residual tension in this area. With each cycle, you notice it becomes easier and easier to release and relax each muscle group... Now again, bring your awareness to the jaw and "tense" and hold for one ... two ... three ... four..., and release ... inhaling through the nose and exhaling through the mouth, relaxing even more with each breath.

Now, bring your awareness to the facial muscles. When I say "tense," please tense the muscles in the face by furrowing the brow and squeezing the muscles together as if you've just eaten a very tart, sour lemon and holding for a count of four seconds and then release. Ready... So, with your awareness in the face now tense and hold for one ... two ... three ... four..., and "release" all the muscles in the face. Notice the difference between a tense muscle and a relaxed muscle as you go through the process. Remembering to inhale through the nose and exhale through the mouth, releasing any residual tension in the face. With each cycle, you notice it becomes easier and easier to release and relax each muscle group... Now again, bring your awareness to the face, "tense" and hold for one ... two ... three ... face..., and release ... inhaling through the nose and exhaling through the mouth, relaxing even more with each breath.

When you have finished, you can open your eyes if they were closed and return your full attention back to the room, ready to move forward with the rest of your day.

Appendix B.
Additional Resources

Here are some additional helpful resources if you would like to explore some of these topics in more detail. This list is a compilation of some of the best research I have collected over 20-plus years of working with clients to become resilient to stressors, grow their confidence, improve health, build intuition, become better parents and love their careers.

Note that printed websites may change over time. I update resources frequently on my website, www.drbarbaracox.com.

Beck, A.T. (1976). *Cognitive therapy and the emotional disorders.* New York: International Universities Press.

Beck, A.T. (1991). Cognitive therapy: A 30-year retrospective. *American Psychologist, 46,* 368–375.

Benson, H. (1975). *The relaxation response.* New York: Morrow.

Brown, G.W., Ehrolchain, N., & Harris, T. (1975). Social class and psychiatric disturbance among women in urban populations. *Sociology, 9,* 225–254.

Callahan, R. (1985). *Five-minute phobia cure.* Wilmington, DE: Enterprise Publishing, Inc.

Christensen, A.J., Turner, C.W., Slaughter, J.R., & Holman, J.M. (1989). Perceived family support as a moderator of psychological well-being in end-stage renal disease. *Journal of Behavioral Medicine, 12,* 3, 249–265.

Cohen, S., & Hoberman, H.N. (1983). Positive events and social supports as buffers of life change stress. *Journal of Applied Social Psychology, 13,* 2, 99–125.

Cox, B.J., Nicassio, P., Greenberg, M.A., & Davis, R. (1999). A biopsychosocial model of depression in adults with cerebral palsy. Poster presented at the 20th Annual Society of Behavioral Medicine, Nashville, Tennessee.

Additional Resources

Davis, M., Eshelman, E.R., & McKay, M. (1996). *The relaxation and stress reduction workbook*. Oakland, CA: New Harbinger Publications Inc.

Dean, A., Lin, N., & Ensel, W. (1981). The epidemiological significance of social support systems in depression. In R.G. Simons (Ed.), *Research community and mental health, vol. 2*. Greenwich, CT: JAI Press. 77–109.

Douglass, L.G. (1997). Reciprocal support in the context of cancer: perspectives of the patient and spouse. *Oncology Nursing Forum, 24*, 9, 1529–1536.

Druckerman, P. (2012). *Bringing up bebe: One American mother discovers the wisdom of French parenting*. New York: Penguin.

Esch, T., Fricchione, G., & Stefano, G. (2003). The therapeutic use of relaxation response in stress-related diseases. *Medical Science Monitor, 9*, 2, 23–34.

Gach, M.R. (1990). *Acupressure's potent points: A guide to self-care for common ailments*. New York: Bantam Books.

Gallo, F.P. (1999). *Energy psychology: Explorations at the interface of energy, cognition, behavior and health*. New York: CRC Press.

Greenberg, M.A., & Stone, A.A. (1990). Writing about disclosed versus undisclosed traumas: Health and mood effects. *Health Psychology, 9*, 114–115.

Greenberg, M.A., & Stone, A.A. (1992). Emotional disclosure about traumas and health: Effects of previous disclosure and trauma severity. *Journal of Personality and Social Psychology, 63*, 75–84.

Greenberg, M.A., Wortman, C.B., & Stone, A.A. (1996). Emotional expression and physical health: Revising traumatic memories or fostering self-regulation? *Journal of Personality & Social Psychology, 71*, 558–602.

Holmes, T.H., & Rahe, R.H. (1967). The social readjustment rating scale. *Journal of Psychosomatic Research, 11*, 2, 213–218.

House, J.S. (1981). *Work stress and social support*. Reading, MA: Addison/Wesley.

Hyman, R.B., Feldman, H.R., Harris, R.B., Levine, R.F., & Malloy, G.B. (1989). The effects of relaxation training on clinical symptoms: A meta-analysis. *Nursing Research, 38*, 216–220.

Jacobson, E. (1938). *Progressive relaxation*. Chicago: University of Chicago Press.

Kanner, A.D., Coyne, J.C., Schaefer, C., & Lazarus, R.S. (1981). The comparison of two modes of stress management: Daily hassles and uplifts versus major life events. *Journal of Behavioral Medicine, 4*, 1–39.

Lambrou, P., & Pratt, G. (2000). *Acupressure for the emotions: Instant emotional healing*. New York: Broadway Books.

Lang, E.V., Benotsch, E.G., Fick, L.J., Lutgendorf, S., Berbaum, M.L., Berbaum, K.S., Logan, H., & Spiegel, D. (2000). Adjunctive non-pharmacological analgesia for invasive medical procedures: A randomised trial. *Lancet, 355*, 1486–1490.

Appendix B

Lazarus, R.S., & Folkman, S. (1984). *Stress, appraisal, and, coping.* New York: Springer.

Lepore, S.J., & Greenberg, M.A. (2002). Mending broken hearts: Effects of expressive writing on mood, cognitive processing, social adjustment, and health following a relationship breakup. *Psychology and Health, 17,* 547–560.

Lepore, S.J., Greenberg, M.A., Bruno, M., & Smyth, J.M. (2002). Expressive writing and health: Self-regulation of emotion-related experience, physiology, and behavior. In S.J. Lepore & J.M. Smyth (Eds.), *The writing cure.* Washington, D.C.: American Psychological Association.

Littlefield, C.H., Rodin, G.N., Murray, N.A., & Craven, J.L. (1990). Influence of functional impairment and social support on depressive symptoms in persons with diabetes. *Health Psychology, 9,* 6, 737–749.

Naparstek, B. (1994). *Staying well with guided imagery.* New York: Warner Books, Inc.

National Center for Complementary and Alternative Medicine (n.d.). https://nccih.nih.gov/health/acupuncture/introduction.

Parker, J.C. (1995). Stress management. In P.M. Nicassio & T.W. Smith (Eds.), *Managing chronic illness: A biopsychosocial perspective.* Washington, D.C.: American Psychological Association.

Pennebaker, J.W. (1997). *Opening up: The healing power of expressing emotions, revised edition.* New York: Guilford Press.

Pinker, S. (1994). *The language instinct.* New York: Morrow.

Schaffer, M. (1982). *Life after stress.* New York: Plenum.

Seyle, H. (1946). The general adaptation syndrome and diseases of adaptation. *Journal of Clinical Endocrinology, 6,* 117–230.

Seyle, H. (1956). *The stress of life.* New York: McGraw-Hill.

Smith, E.E., Nolen-Hoeksema, S., Fredrickson, B.L., Loftus, G.R., Bem, D.J., & Maren, S. (2003). *Atkinson & Hilgard's introduction to psychology.* Belmont, CA: Thompson Wadsworth Inc.

Stanny, B. (2005). *Overcoming underearning: A five-step plan to a richer life.* New York: First Collins.

Turner, R.J. (1983). Direct, indirect and moderating effects of social support upon psychological stress and associated conditions. In H.B. Kaplan (Ed.), *Psychological stress: Trends in theory and research.* New York: New York Academic Press. 105–155.

Vygotsky, L.S. (1934/1962). *Thought and language.* E. Haufmann and G. Vaker (Eds. and Trans.) Cambridge: MIT Press.

Yapko, M.D. (1995). *Essentials of hypnosis.* New York: Brunner/Mazel.

Index

Index